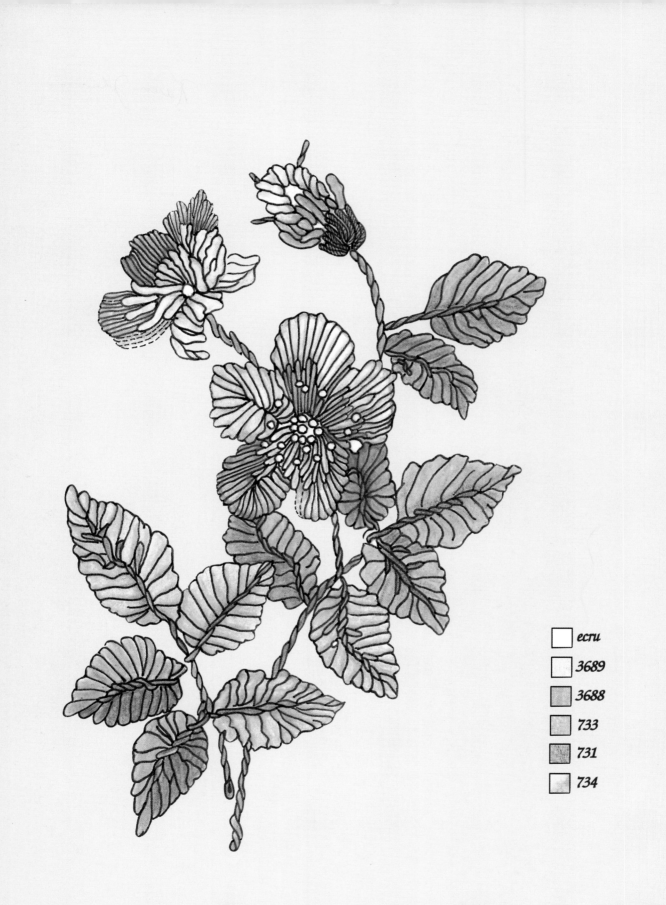

ecru
3689
3688
733
731
734

TREASURY OF CRAZY QUILT STITCHES

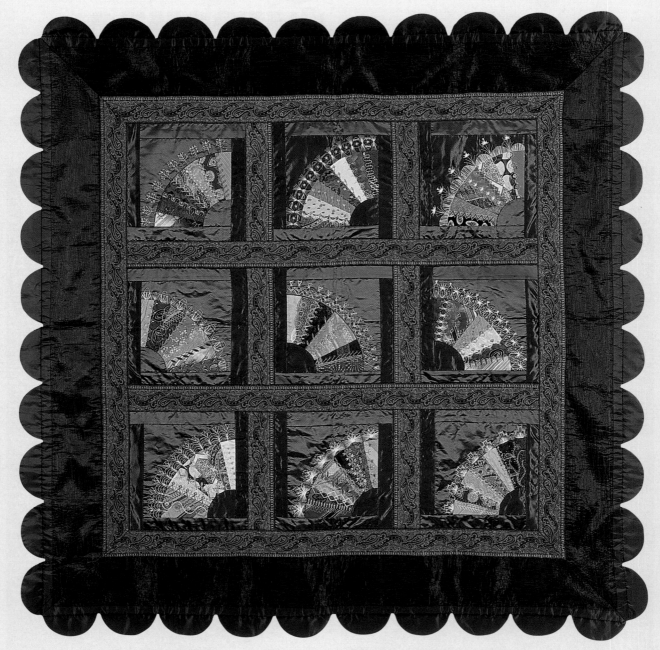

"Daddy's Ties Are MOMMY'S Now!" by the author, Omaha, Nebraska, ©1996

Treasury
of
Crazyquilt Stitches

A Comprehensive Guide to
Traditional Hand Embroidery
Inspired by Antique Crazyquilts

by Carole Samples

Located in Paducah, Kentucky, the American Quilter's Society (AQS) is dedicated to promoting the accomplishments of today's quilters. Through its publications and events, AQS strives to honor today's quiltmakers and their work and to inspire future creativity and innovation in quiltmaking.

EDITOR: ROBERT J. MARTIN
ASSISTANT EDITOR: BARBARA SMITH
BOOK DESIGN: CASSIE A. ENGLISH
COVER DESIGN: MICHAEL BUCKINGHAM
PHOTOGRAPHY: CHARLES R. LYNCH
HAND-DRAWN GRAPHICS: CAROLE SAMPLES

Library of Congress Cataloging-in-Publication Data

Samples, Carole K. Parks
    Treasury of crazy quilt stitches: a comprehensive guide to traditional hand embroidery inspired by antique crazyquilts / by Carole K. Parks Samples.
                            p.   cm.
    Includes bibliographical references (p. 220-223).
    ISBN 1-57432-728-3
    1. Embroidery Patterns. 2. Crazy quilts. I. Title.
TT771.P27   1999
746.44'041--dc21   99-37103
                                                CIP

Additional copies of this book may be ordered from the American Quilter's Society, PO Box 3290, Paducah, KY 42002-3290 @ $26.95. Add $2.00 for postage and handling.

Copyright © 1999, Carole Samples

The Dedication

The Treasury of Crazyquilt Stitches requires a six-part dedication as I express my respect for and love of family, past, present, and future, and my profound gratitude to my "forever friends:"

To Mary Jane Brown Greene, my maternal great-grandmother and the first generation of womenfolk in the family to establish a successful home-based business (she operated her small town's only laundry at the turn of the century); Eileene Smith Greene, my maternal grandmother and sole proprietress of a long-time, semi-secret antiques shop which occupied every room in her house save one, keeper of the only telephone on her block throughout the 1930s, and expert on all things porcelain; Sallie Bates Henderson, my aunt, a legendary caterer and cook who kept a kosher kitchen and collected all the things I love; and Mary E. Greene Parks, my mother, who taught us by word and example how to achieve success and how always to hope for life's greater promises;

To the members in good standing of The Crazyquilters' Support Group of Eastern Nebraska, who have inspired and taught me and given their encouragement and time and so much affection to me over the five-plus years of our happy association;

To Lynn Carta Tolles, as great a friend as anyone could ever have, who has been there — here, that is — since my professional beginnings, making much of my progress possible, asking so little while giving so much;

To the late Mary Lou Sayers, quiltmaker extraordinaire and heavenly advocate, who helped me to understand that I must do crazywork, who promoted my teaching career wherever she took her own QUILT-IN-A-DAY™ classes, and who never reminded me that she was first in our large circle to finish a crazyquilt or that her skills were far superior to mine;

To my sons, Chuck and Peter, so gifted and funny and genuinely great-hearted, who constantly amaze me and bring both joy and hope to their parents' lives; and ...

To my grandchildren, yet unborn. I love you already.

The Crazyquilters' Support Group of Eastern Nebraska, photo by Joe Hammeke

The Contents

The Foreword 7

The Preface 8

The Introduction 11

The Gallery 15

PART ONE: THE FUNDAMENTALS 22

Chapter One: One Stitch at a Time 24

    The Six Basic Stitch Groups and Why It Matters 25

    The Primary and Preparatory Stitches of Crazyquilt Embroidery 26

    A Dictionary of Authentic and Original Stitches for Crazyquilts 27

    The Great Pretenders 51

Chapter Two: Applications 54

    . . . But Function Matters, too 55

    Chart: The Nine Functions of Crazyquilt Stitches 57

Chapter Three: From Stitch to Stitchery 58

    The Anatomy of a Stitchery: A Few Necessary Terms 59

Chapter Four: The Art of Linear Stitchery 66

    Multiples and Modifications 67

PART TWO: THE STITCHERIES 72

Chapter One: Straight-Thread-Stitch Designs 74

Chapter Two: Blanket-Stitch & Feather-Stitch Designs 110

Chapter Three: Tied-Stitch & Linked-Stitch Designs 126

Chapter Four: Knotted-Stitch & Coiled-Stitch Designs 136

Chapter Five: Combination-Technique-Stitch Designs 138

Chapter Six: Laced/Threaded-Stitch & Woven-Stitch Designs 142

Chapter Seven: Plain & Fancy Embellishers 146

Chapter Eight: Patch Pictures: Music for the Eyes 160

Chapter Nine: Doodle-Stitch Designs 186

Chapter Ten: Spiders' Webs: A Comprehensive View of a Traditional Motif 190

Chapter Eleven: Alphabets & Words: Embroidered Writing 198

Chapter Twelve: Texturing 208

The Acknowledgments 214

The Biography 218

A Crazyquilter's Reading List 220

The Foreword

When studying the countless embroidery stitch combinations found on old crazyquilts, my sole focus was the stitch variations found on their seams. But I was not unmindful of another study to be made of the symbols, motifs, and pictures that almost always appear on crazyquilts.

I often wished that someone would come along to take on this subject. And now, happily we have Treasury of Crazyquilt Stitches by Carole Samples. In this book, her careful illustrations include not only linear combinations based on the important stitches used in ages past, but also a vast number of those other designs that go beyond the embroidery covering the seams of crazyquilts onto the quilt bodies.

This book is full of ideas that are bound to excite the imagination of any modern-day stitcher.

Dorothy Bond, author of Crazy Quilt Stitches

Dorothy Bond and her legendary "little brown book"

The front cover and an open page in Dorothy Bond's book, *Crazy Quilt Stitches*

The Preface

I wish I could remember the moment I first saw a crazyquilt. I'd love to trace my affinity for and mild obsession with them to a particular date or experience — a quilt-show encounter, perhaps, or an old magazine article. Somewhere and some time ago, I came upon A Patchworthy Apparel Book by Jean Wells and Marinda Anderson. That was one of the magical moments in my creative life, as from its very covers I saw laces, ribbons, colors, and stitches used in ways I'd never imagined.

Although I continued to make the traditional scrap-look quilts from my precious stash of 1970s mini-prints, as so many of us did in the mid-1980s, I selfishly spent many, many hours with the great books of that decade (or so they were to me): Crazy Quilts (my primary textbook), Crazy Quilt Stitches (my dictionary of designs), The Complete Book of Crazy Patchwork (the marvelous book that finally made feather stitching intelligible to me), Crazy Quilt Handbook (the book I wish I had written), and America's Glorious Quilts (filled with inspiration).

How could I not be content, so happily immersed in the hundreds of quilts old and new, the beautiful project ideas, and the thousands of stitch combinations I had at my disposal? And I began to collect things — mostly perle cotton and shiny rayon threads, pretty pieces of polyester-and-cotton-blend cloth, and short lengths of flat laces and satin ribbons in all my favorite colors. I even found a real job at the world-famous mercantile establishment in my city, where I enthusiastically spent most of my very small salary to buy ever more interesting threads, more books, specialty notions, and bits of gorgeous fabrics originally intended for professional costumer designers. It was by that time 1988. Needless to say, I was smitten.

But I wasn't ready. Timid souls so often find it difficult to begin the doing of a new thing, even when the desired outcome or product is necessary to our happiness and well-being (or is just plain wonderful). The problem: there was no one to show me how to actually make a crazyquilt, no person among my acquaintances to tell me where to start and how to proceed to a successful end. Somehow I would have to reach the point where the dreaming and the doing, the need to create beauty, and the fear of wasting time and resources all merged into one moment of courage and decision when I could make the triumphant leap from cowardly perfectionism to — well, I think you get the picture!

Now, if I were not absolutely certain that there are at least 5,000 of you who know exactly what I am talking about, I would have spared the rest of my readers such a personal revelation. But I have a point to make, so please bear with me.

Believe it or not, there really was a moment of decision. It happened as I was straightening the needlework aisle at the store one day, something I had done dozens of times before. This time, all those bolts of even-weave linens and other cross-stitch fabrics suggested the most fantastic cure for even the most serious case of procrastination: samplers.

I seemed to comprehend the ideal solution in an instant, as I recalled how countless numbers of young ladies were taught to do the most elegant stitchery by means of their practice pieces. Upon these (often homespun) lengths of cloth were worked the traditional European symbols and motifs that decorated their lives. What a supremely simple yet perfect device for learning their essential stitches — or for learning mine! It was so obvious: "If happy little girls could ply" their needles daily, "why, oh, why couldn't I?"

I designed and worked my Sampler One in a month's worth of spare time and proudly displayed The Twenty-one Basic Stitches of Crazyquilt Embroidery in November 1988. The 18-count Davosa cloth had made it so easy to see exactly where to place the needle, and I gradually overcame my fear of making uneven stitches as I worked. It wasn't authentic, liberated crazy-work stitching, but it was a start. I was learning the fundamentals of my chosen craft in the only way that made sense to the left-brained aspect of my creative mind, and I shall be forever grateful to my needlework angel for the inspiration that gave me the courage to begin at last.

I have written Treasury of Crazyquilt Stitches for people like me who need a lot of help! Whether or not you have a teacher to guide you, whether you are a self-starting, I'll-try-anything-once kind of person with a string of completed projects behind you, or a timid soul whose anxieties about failure and the unknown and not being perfect enough have limited your creative output, you are going to find in this book so much encouragement and so many answers to your questions about our subject, that you will simply have to put some stitches on something very soon. When you are ready, this book will be here as a loving substitute for a living person who knows exactly what to do, helping you to realize that it's not about perfection. It's all about making as much beauty as you can for yourself and others. The endeavor asks only that you believe in yourself and in the book before you and that you give yourself permission to make mistakes until you have mastered all of the necessary techniques — and you will.

And if ever the learning or the doing becomes difficult, if you find yourself pressured (and tempted) by the desire to create a masterpiece before you know how, just say to yourself: "Carole Samples took a long time, but she finally figured all of this out. She knew only seven stitches when she started. Now she can do more than a hundred of them, and rather nicely, too. If she were here, she would remind me of the lessons her samplers taught her: to practice my stitches, to practice patience, and to practice perseverance until the crazyquilt of my dreams is a beautiful reality. Carole didn't give up her passion to make her quilts even when it wasn't easy or fun. She kept trying until she got it right. Now she has some lovely things to show for her efforts. If she can do it, so can I!" And that is my point!

My first three crazyquilt projects date back to 1986. In those early years, I resorted to several desperate measures, such as the use of — dare I say the word? — fusibles. At the time, it seemed truly creative; and besides, I hadn't yet figured out how the piecing is actually done. The important thing is, from these humble efforts, a career was born. Isn't that something!

From the very beginning, I followed my own first rule of procedure for timid souls: I started small. Little by little, skill by skill, I learned enough to share with others. It is, therefore, with immense gratitude to every student, past and future, and to all my beloved friends with whom I collaborate so often and so merrily, that I offer my first book, a gift of celebratory reading to anyone who may profit from the contents of these pages.

There is more beauty to be found in the work of a woman's hands than anyone can know and much joy in the beholding thereof. May my words and pictures inspire every reader to make something beautiful and to find much joy in the doing.

The Introduction

Most crazyquilters don't need rules, but...

The Treasury of Crazyquilt Stitches has evolved from a small hand-illustrated workbook that I developed for students in my "Absolute-Beginners' Crazyquilt Patchwork and Stitchery" classes. Those 22 stapled pages were filled, for the most part, with a modest assortment of seamwork designs I had created, although I also included several more impressive examples from other sources. I sold more than 200 copies of the expanded 40-page version over the years since then, building much-needed confidence with each sale. By 1995 I had begun to believe I just might have something that other crazyquilters would be happy to see.

You have before you my finished work, the product of four additional years in which 40 pages grew and were revised countless times, it seemed to me, until at last there was far too much material for a single book. A decision was made early on that there would be no projects in the Treasury. Instead, the subject matter in this long-awaited volume will comprise a study of the one thing I know most about — the traditional, nineteenth-century mode of crazyquilt embroidery, with emphasis on the most popular stitches used to create the thousands of seamwork and patch-decoration designs on the fancy crazyquilts of that era. My intention is two-fold: I wish to remind modern-day crazyquilters of the perfectly lovely results that are possible with thread work alone and to present essential, never-before-published information that will explain exactly how the hundred-year-old motifs we so admire were invented.

Also, the determination not to include instructions on how to do the individual stitches was dictated by the number of pages available to me and by the fact that so many outstanding books on contemporary crazywork and general embroidery contain beautifully illustrated lessons on this subject. If you do not already own or have access to one or more of the hand-embroidery textbooks, I hope you will acquire one very soon and that you will use it.

Within these pages you will find many references to numbers of things; namely, the Six Basic Stitch Groups, the Primary and Preparatory Stitches, and the Nine Functions of Crazyquilt Stitches, for starters. In fact, the Treasury is organized in such a way that these concepts are defined and treated chapter by chapter. One of the very best features of the book is my Dictionary of Authentic and Original Stitches for Crazyquilts, an exclusive 24-page illustrated listing of the 48 primary stitches I selected for this volume, along with 1,700 of their variant forms. For the first time to my knowledge, 800 "embellishers" have been catalogued separately in Part Two.

As a matter of interest, embellishers as a group are one of the five categories of crazyquilt embroidery designs which I refer to as "stitcheries" (pgs. 146 – 207). You are going to see most of what I have discovered about linear stitcheries, which usually are worked along the seams of the patchwork itself; "patch pictures," which are meant to adorn the centers of cloth pieces; writing; and texturing, a special form of whole-patch decoration with stitches, as well. Altogether, I have gathered almost 2,200 designs, most of which are my own creations, including more than 300 simple and complex patch pictures, spot motifs, spiders and their webs, plus one antique and one original alphabet of capital letters. But there is more.

The Treasury of Crazyquilt Stitches is all about looking beneath the surface of every linear design, especially, to really see what Victorian-era crazyquilt makers were doing when they devised each seamwork stitchery. I will introduce you to new terminology and to design concepts that are quite specific to our subject but which may, until now, have remained hidden from plain view, and which have become evident only after the years I have spent studying and dissecting thousands of antique stitch combinations from hundreds of old quilts. Once you review the remarkable findings in Part One, Chapters Three and Four, you may never again look at a complex linear stitchery in the same way.

The same goes for crazyquilt patchwork. Those hours of close encounters with embroidery yielded an unexpected but invaluable discovery that has so greatly enhanced my appreciation of the way pieces of cloth were put together a hundred-plus years ago. As a result, I was able to 32 generic block structures that can be used today to make authentically traditional crazyquilts! Several of these construction formats, as they are called, can be seen in The Gallery, which presents the color portraits of the blocks made especially for this book by friends, colleagues, unknown needle artists, and me.

There is also a Crazyquilter's Reading List , so called because it is not presented in standard bibliography form. Instead, the books' titles are given first, and every book has been coded to help you see its most important contributions or potential applications to crazyquilt making.

As for the extended Acknowledgments, my readers need to realize that very few of us who become professional quilting/needlework/craftwork teachers ever manage such a feat by ourselves. In my case, in addition to all of my students since January 1986, more than 100 individuals were there when I needed a very special favor or commodity or class to complete my understanding or advance my status in some definitive way. "It doth, indeed, take a village ..." And this book, to a great extent, is my way of thanking each person properly for saying "yes" when she or he didn't have to.

One of the first and most essentially involved people I contacted at the outset of this endeavor was Dorothy Bond, author and publisher of *Crazy Quilt Stitches* — the legendary little brown book which must certainly be in every serious crazyquilter's personal library. All of us are more indebted to Mrs. Bond than we can ever say, because she was the first person, I believe, to actually document so many stitcheries (1,052) directly from antique crazyquilts and then to share them with you and me. Her book, along with Penny McMorris's *Crazy Quilts* and Jean Wells's *A Patchworthy Apparel Book* (all of which I found at nearly the same time in my life), were the books that first excited me and made me want to take up crazyquilting right then. Mrs. Bond gave me permission to use primary stitches and embellishers from her book in my own; she sent many design sheets from her vast collection of nineteenth-century facsimile materials; she gave me an 1898 crazyquilt top to love and care for; and she has listened patiently to four years' worth of progress reports and anxieties as I brought the manuscript to completion. Without her, the Treasury would have been very difficult to write, and it surely would have been neither as complete nor as significant.

I began these remarks with a reference to the fact that most of us who love and make and want to make crazyquilts do not require any rules to aid our wholesome undertaking. In fact, generally speaking, it is all of the Rules of Quiltmaking, all of the "finessing unto perfection," that take so much of the fun out of the process of creating a finished quilt. For someone who loves old laces, trims, hankies, buttons, beading, and three-dimensional additives as much as I do while hating everything that has to do with Precision and Matching and symmetrical Balance, only crazyquilt making would do.

It occurs to me that, in addition to amassing a lot of wonderful "software," crazyquilters need three things without question: one, a clear sense of Purpose (the "why-am-I-doing-this?" component of the process); two, some Passion (the driving force from within, which makes finishing things an almost spiritual necessity); and three, Permission. This last prerequisite may be the hardest to come by. Some of us simply need to relax, put all notions of "perfection" or "appropriateness" or "not knowing enough" (for example, about mixing fabrics or colors and about working the various stitches) into a mental throw-away bin, and give ourselves several Permissions: to acquire as many of the lovely materials and necessary supplies (the "software") and tools (the "hardware") as we can afford, to make messes and even leave them where they are when we complete a work session, to waste cloth from time to time, and Permission to not get it right the first (or the second) time!

Spread out your prepared and preselected pieces of cloth, pick up your preferred scissors or rotary slicing implement, take a deep breath, and cut something. (After all, it's only fabric!) Make a patchwork block in colors that delight you. Put some simple stitches on every seam. Then put some stitches upon those stitches. Let the beautiful/whimsical/provocative/primitive/eccentric or otherwise necessary fiber object in your imagination become, slowly over the hours, a stunning reality.

You may also find that a fourth requirement — namely, a Person of Compatible Sensibilities, will help you to focus your creative energies on one project at a time and thus enable you to do that which was not possible before. Working with one or more others is a time-honored way to true accomplishment which should not be underestimated. And a collection of goal-centered friends is one of life's greatest blessings!

Lastly, to the extent that this Treasury of Crazyquilt Stitches can inform your need to know the subtleties and the intricacies of our special type of needlework and to the extent that it encourages your further research into the mysteries and manners of the Victorian crazyquilt tradition, I am very happy to provide one primary source of inspiration and ideas. There must come a moment, however, when everyone has to put all books aside for a while so that the product so long desired might be brought into being.

It is my sincere wish that you will use all of the information presented in these pages to enhance the creative processes in yourself until, finally, you feel confident enough to design and work thousands of stitch combinations and "patch pictures." Your original stitcheries as well as every item you produce will become your own unique body of work and your special artistic legacy to the rest of us.

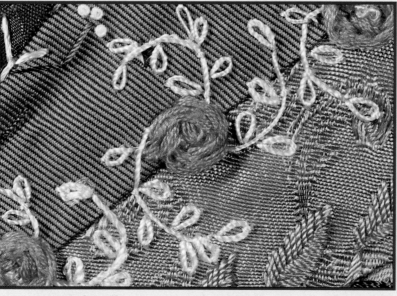

Detail of "Daddy's Ties Are MOMMY'S Now!" by the author, 1996

The Gallery

Designer/maker: unknown 1900 – 1910

Details: The "Rocky Road To Kansas" block pattern was embellished in the manner of a fairly fancy crazyquilt on this sixteen-star, machine-pieced gem. I partially restitched a few of the damaged linear designs in closely-matched threads and colors. Other blocks contain warm and/or cool browns, a brown/black gingham check, a blue/gray/brown flannel plaid, and dull mustard and/or butterscotch-colored strips – a comparatively unappealing palette, were it not for the warm red "diamonds" which separate the pieced elements.

1. Designer/maker: Kathleen E. Smith, Omaha, NE (1999)
Details: Kathy accepted my challenge to work in wool cloth for the first time, piecing the block in an authentically antique, irregular format which is still recognizably a "Log Cabin" variation. The bamboo hand screen comes from page 177. All of the stitcheries were worked in high-contrasting colors that are perfect against the dark, manly mix of fabrics. (Notice how each adjacent pair of solid or tweedy strips is balanced in the same round by a pair of plaid strips of the same basic color – one of the choices which makes this preplanned block so successful.)

2. Designer/maker: author (1993)
Details: This quarter-circle fan was pieced using Georgia Bonesteel's freezer-paper-template method. Threads are cotton and rayon floss, sizes 8 and 12 perle cotton, and size D silk buttonhole twist of happy memory.

3. Designer/Maker: Lynn E. Tolles, Omaha, NE (1998)
Details: Four colors alternate among the twelve spokes of the wheel. Heavy, ribbed faille was cut in a ring and a circle to form the rim and hub of the center patchwork; both are hand appliquéd in place. Believe it or not, this arrangement is a genuine antique crazyquilt block structure. Lynn uses each fabric only once in a quilt, and she mixes every weight and fiber of thread.

4. Designer/maker: author (1992)
Details: All of the threadwork is in one or two strands of cotton floss except for a golden metallic used on two designs. The linear stitcheries are all from Basic Stitch Group One except for the triple-feather stitching. The fusible-appliqué motifs were added to hide less-than-perfect piecing; these were also enhanced with black-ink outlining.

5. Designer/maker: author (1997)
Details: Two satin ribbons are stacked and couched with a complex design. Narrow ribbons hide three seams. Size 14 clear glass seed beads and little bugle beads team with the stitchery. A 2mm silk ribbon zigzags across a seam – a rare but authentic antique-crazy quilt application.

6. Designer/maker: author (1992)
Designs: The stacked-fly-stitch designs and the chain-stitched hearts (outlines only) were worked in a doubled silk sewing thread. Several fine examples of linear stitcheries from Basic Stitch Group Three are presented. The butterfly has both satin and Kensington stitch elements. This was my second crazywork block.

7. Designer/maker: author (1996)
Details: Stem-stitched scallops in size 12 ecru perle cotton

form the needlework lace edging. The roses are done in Marlitt rayon.

8. Designer/maker: author (1996)
Details: Mock sheaf-stitch clusters are embellished with large-scale, couched detached chain stitches to create an original curved lace – a complex, time-consuming, but deceptively easy linear construction. Harder to do were the zigzag-stitch and the broadband, zigzagging-blanket-stitch designs. The cretan catch stitches are shadowed with wide fly stitches, while large cross stitches perform the same task for the zigzag stitches. This fan block and the one above were both sewn using foundation piecing for the blades and blind-hem appliqué, with the curved taffeta pieces stitched on top of the blades' raw edges.

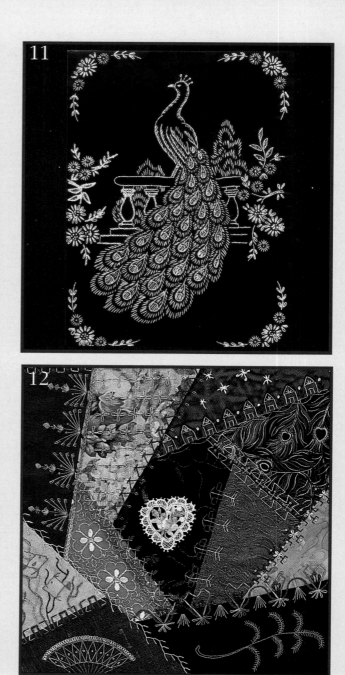

9. Designer/maker: author (1997 – 1999)
Details: This is the other half of panel #5 on page 17. I added two antique trims, both at the top of the block, and two modern ones, along with three couched ribbons, silvery and black/golden metallic threads, bugle beads, couched ribbons, and glass seed beads. Two selvages were purposely left uncovered; can you find them?

10. Designer/maker: author (1993)
Details: Most of the stitcheries are intermediate level time and are worked in size D silk buttonhole twist as well as Marlitt rayon floss and size 8 perle cotton threads. By alternating the patterned cotton and poly/satin blades with dark taffeta strips, I could showcase my stitching to full advantage. (The spider who lives on this block was vacationing in Ireland at last report.)

11. Details: A gift from a sister guild member, this figurative embroidery piece was done in three or four strands of white floss (now somewhat less than pristine) on dress-weight black satin. The peacock was one of the most popular, and one of the most complex and difficult to render well in thread or paint, of all the Victorian-era birds. This simplified design, however, requires far more patience and perseverance than skill to complete successfully.

12. Designer/maker: Kathleen E. Smith (1999)
Details: Threads of nearly every available type were chosen to mimic the fabrics' autumn palette; bright blue, turquoise, and the bright yellow portion of the variegated chain stitch add needed contrast rather than perfect balance. The fish, row houses, and hearts belong to a special type of stitchery I call "doodle-stitch" designs.

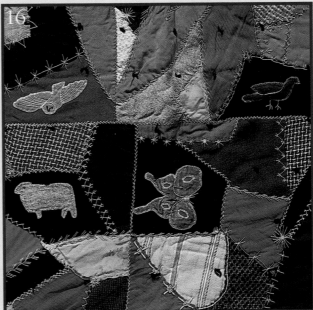

13. Designer/maker: author (1995)

Details: My full-circle web is stitched in silver-metallic thread with straight, couched turns and three extra anchoring threads to hold it. I cut a clamshell motif from a beautiful Joan Kessler print and blind-hem appliquéd it. The pink triple feather stitching was done in four strands of cotton floss with size 8 perle cotton knots. The golden fan is in silk buttonhole twist. To my eye, the commercially tie-dyed cloth in the center makes the block.

14. Designer/maker: Betty Pillsbury, NY (1998)

Details: Many techniques and designs worthy of a closer look are on this lovely block. The needle artist stitched her initial on a dense velveteen patch, not an easy task, and her spider's web is as delicate as I have ever seen. The mix of simple and complex patch pictures is both instructive and pleasing.

15. Designer/maker: Mary Lou Sayers, Clarkson, NE (1997)

Details: The elegant, almost somber block is one of 20 that "ML" pieced for her second crazyquilt. Wherever she found a suitable printed or woven motif, she emphasized it with dainty texturing stitches. You can see this better, perhaps, in the enlargement on page 208. Mary Lou was also a gifted designer of medallion-style spot motifs and complex fans, never repeating the same one twice.

16. Provenance: unknown, dated Jan. 5, 1903

Details: A four block area from the folk-art style crazyquilt on page 20 reveals the fact that its blocks are not uniform in size, but vary in width from 13 to 15 inches. The tiniest straight feather stitching, barely ⅛ inch to ³⁄₁₆ inch wide, trims every block-to-block seam. There are nine primary stitches on this quilt that I have not seen on any other, indelible proof of the quiltmaker's inventiveness and sense of adventure!

Designer/maker: unknown, dated Jan. 5, 1903

Details: A wonderful tribute to the world of its maker, this uncommon utility crazyquilt features what must have been one woman's favorite winged and four-legged companions, best-loved stitches, and heaviest woolen leftovers. Among the usual red, red-orange/rust, brown, dark blue, black, gray, and dirty-pink fabrics you'd expect to find, there is an occasional violet patch with cotton-twist threads in a narrow range of light colors, including lavender. The fabrics are far from beautiful, the embroidery is not refined, the palette, less than interesting. Still, it is my quaint, humble, homely treasure. Every time I look at it, it makes me smile.

▨	3688
▨	799
▨	402
▨	3689
▨	307
▨	703
▨	471
▨	562
▨	996
▨	3045
▨	3031

Design from Mittie Barrier Crazyquilt (see p. 170 for more information).
Used by permission of Catherine B. Shoe of Kentucky, granddaughter of the maker.

Part One

The Fundamentals

Detail from antique wool and cotton quilt, maker unknown, 1900 – 1910

Chapter One
One Stitch at a Time

"Sampler One," by the author, 1988

The Six Basic Stitch Groups and Why It Matters

I have yet to meet a quiltmaker or needlecrafter who is self-taught. On the contrary, I cannot imagine how different, how much emptier, my life would be today if it were not for the extraordinary design and research work done by a small group of very gifted women. From their indispensable books, many of us first became acquainted with the art of the needle and, in time, with something called a "crazyquilt." It is largely because of their love for cloth, thread, and all things beautiful, and because they and others have so generously shared their knowledge and discoveries with us over these past 65 years that the needle arts, including quilting, continue to be practiced, taught, and perfected today. Nearly everything I know about crazyquilt making, I owe to them.

All of the ideas and techniques I learned had to be arranged, for the sake of memory, into a logical, easy-to-access system, and upon this system I was able to structure the curriculum I still use to teach crazyquilt stitchery. From the most general to the most specific fact, here are the relevant data needed to make our subject more understandable:

1. The kind of stitching we do is generically known as "surface embroidery" and as "free-style embroidery." Under this very large umbrella are hundreds of named, hand-worked stitches, not to mention the thousands of original and authentic antique-quilt stitches that do not have names.

2. In spite of their number, however, there are only two methods for defining and arranging the individual stitches into a logical system: (a) according to formation — how the stitches are made, and (b) according to function — how each stitch is used on the cloth.

   The main drawback to using function as an organizing system is the fact that 47 of the 48 primary stitches can be used for two or more decorative purposes. Obviously, it would be impossible to assign each stitch to only one function category except, perhaps, to try to agree on each individual stitch's most important, most frequent use, and classify each one accordingly.

3. Because it provides the simplest and most logical way to learn all of the stitches, the formation approach was chosen for this book. Luckily, Mariska Karasz had already done the difficult work of classifying many hand-embroidery stitches by this means in her ground-breaking book, Adventures in Stitches (1949).

4. Modifying Mariska's almost perfect plan, I organized my 48 primary crazyquilt stitches into six basic groups: Group One, the Straight-Thread Stitches; Group Two, the Blanket and Feather Stitches; Group Three, the Chained and Tied Stitches; Group Four, the Knotted and Coiled Stitches; Group Five, the Combination-Technique Stitches; and Group Six, the Laced/Threaded and Woven Stitches.

It may or may not be coincidental, but the stitches most often seen on crazyquilts come from Group One, the second most frequently used stitches are found in Group Two, and so on. Group One contains 20 of the 48 primary stitches, by far the largest number of any basic stitch group. One could conceivably create a masterpiece crazyquilt with seamwork embroidery designs from this first category of stitches exclusively, so varied are its possibilities.

The Primary and Preparatory Stitches of Crazyquilt Embroidery

The difficult decision regarding which of the more than 100 excellent choices would finally become my list of 50 ideal stitches for contemporary crazyquilts was, in the end, based on two important factors: First, I wanted to include the most popular stitches that were used on antique quilts, and second, it seemed appropriate to add a small number of stitches that I did not encounter on any of the quilts I have seen but whose similarity to the traditional stitches makes each of them a natural candidate for this book.

I am very pleased that Treasury of Crazyquilt Stitches presents not only the 50 basic stitches that are perfect for today's crazywork but that it also gives many variations of the named, universally recognized forms of those basic stitches. There is not sufficient space in one volume for every known version of every multiple-version stitch (such as the blanket stitch), nor could I discover all of them myself, but this chapter contains 1,746 authentic crazyquilt stitches, a number arrived at by combining the 48 primary stitches with their 1,698 variant forms. As many stitches as could fit into 24 pages are featured, more than there are in any other publication written specifically for crazyquilters.

I would like to explain the technical terminology I used to introduce this chapter. In the broadest possible sense, traditionally, there are only two kinds of surface embroidery stitches: the majority, which decorate cloth in some way, and those few which prepare other stitches to be decorative. Thus, the first 48 stitches on our master list are "primary" because they are used, always, to directly embroider the seams and patches of our crazyquilting, while the last two stitches are "preparatory," intended for use as outlining and padding stitches, respectively, and will always be completely covered by the satin stitches they enhance. These preparatory stitches, No. 49, split stitch, and No. 50, seed stitch, are not shown in the Dictionary; they are illustrated on p. 201 in Illus. 11-3 and Illus. 11-4, respectively.

Whenever a named stitch has one or more generic versions, I assigned a lower-case letter to each major variation and either noted its commonly accepted name, if it has one, or invented a simple, descriptive name for it, such as scalloping fly stitch or clamshell blanket stitch. Several exceptions were inevitable; for instance, stitch No. 1 contains so many different forms that its 14 subdivisions are lettered rather than each individual stitch being numbered. There are also examples of primary stitches in the Dictionary that are clustered or mirror imaged. These are meant to be stitched as they are drawn: either continuously along a seam or as self-contained units repeating at close intervals along a line (see pages 61, 62, and 67 – 71).

A Dictionary of Authentic and Original Stitches for Crazyquilts
Basic Stitch Group One – Stitches 1 – 20

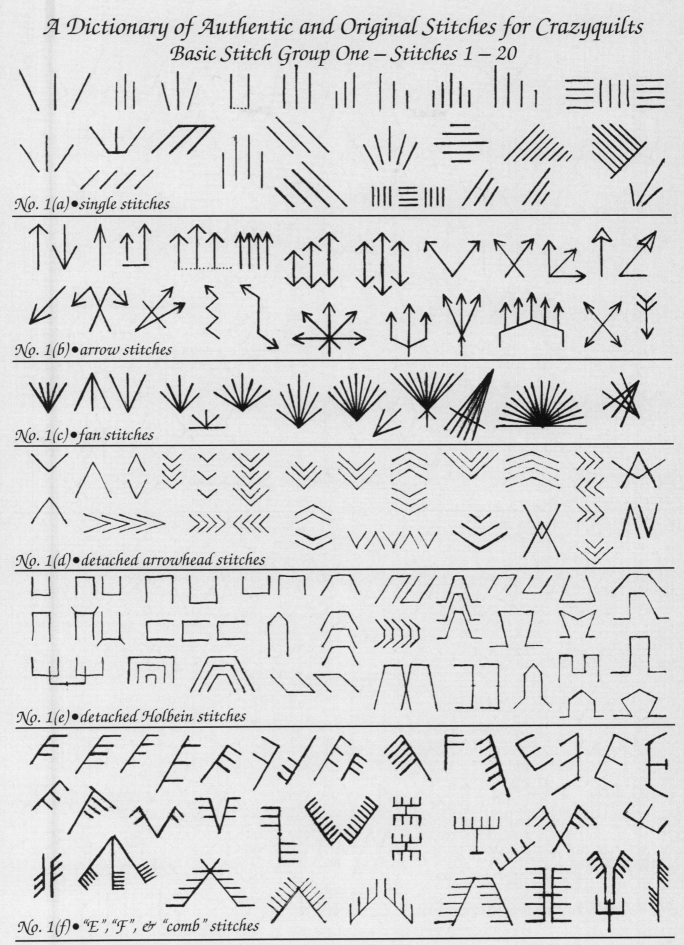

No. 1(a)•single stitches

No. 1(b)•arrow stitches

No. 1(c)•fan stitches

No. 1(d)•detached arrowhead stitches

No. 1(e)•detached Holbein stitches

No. 1(f)•"E", "F", & "comb" stitches

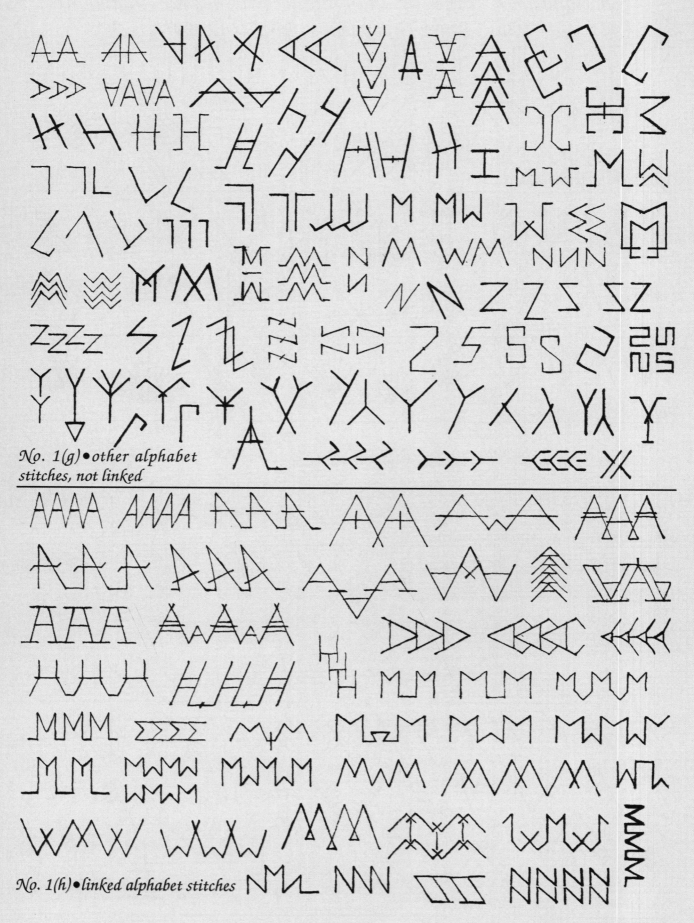

No. 1(g) • other alphabet stitches, not linked

No. 1(h) • linked alphabet stitches

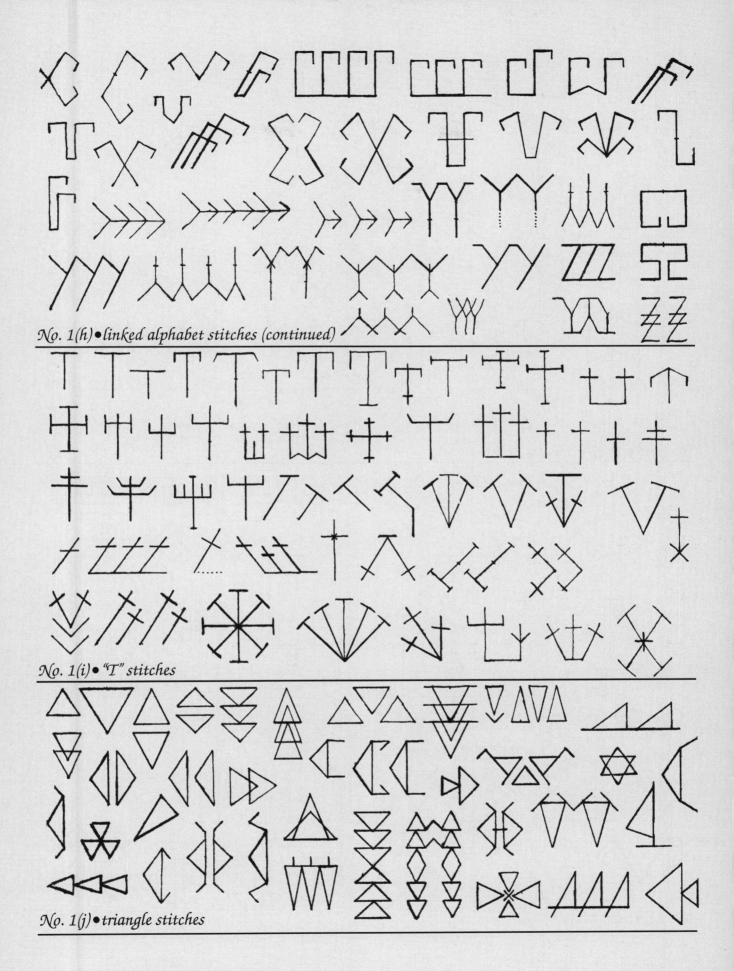

No. 1(h)•linked alphabet stitches (continued)

No. 1(i)• "T" stitches

No. 1(j)•triangle stitches

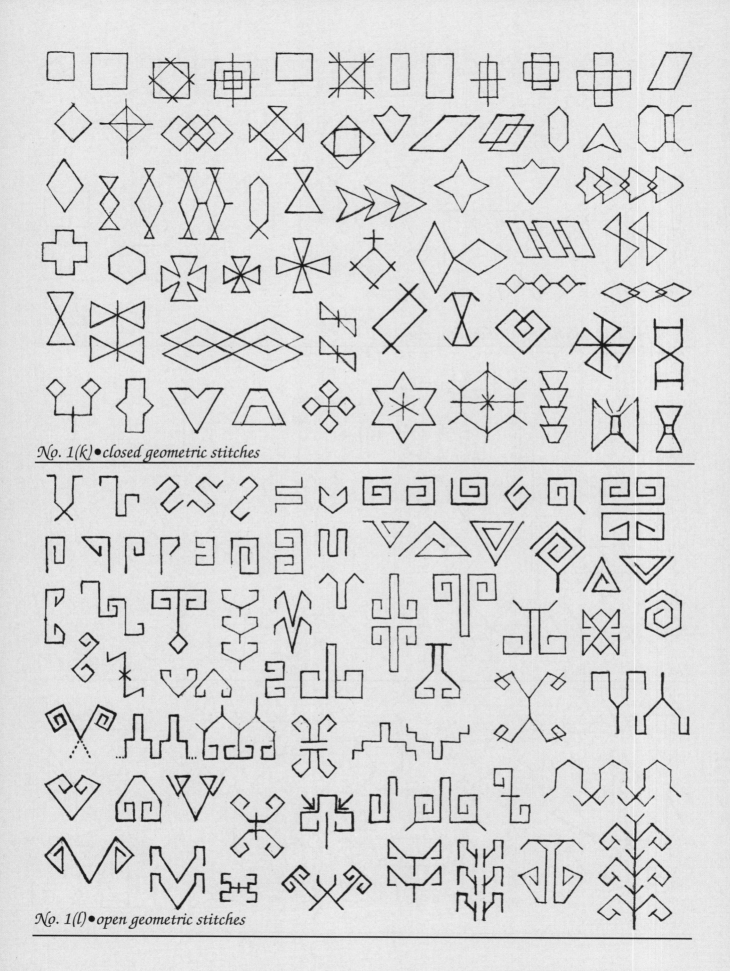

No. 1(k) • closed geometric stitches

No. 1(l) • open geometric stitches

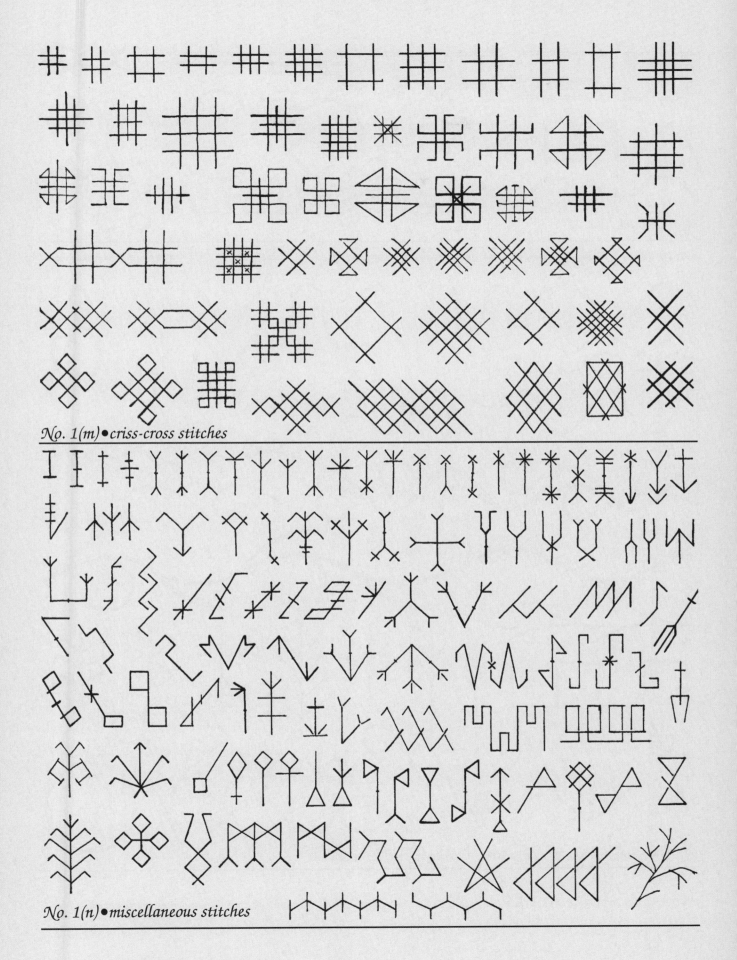

No. 1(m)•criss-cross stitches

No. 1(n)•miscellaneous stitches

No. 2 • *backstitches*

No. 3 • *stem stitches & composites (straight stitches added)*

Note: *Backstitch and stem stitch are virtually — but not absolutely — interchangeable. (The former is the better choice for tight curves and short lines.) Both stitches perform most of the outlining ("drawing" and "writing") on crazyquilts.*

No. 4 • cross stitches

No. 5 • star stitches

No. 6 • snowflake stitches

Note: All of these stitches are variant forms of the common cross stitch. Snowflake stitches are star stitches with two-stitch or three-stitch clusters attached to both ends of the four main stitches, or legs, of each star. Use only one thread color for one entire repeat of each primary stitch (as each one is shown above).

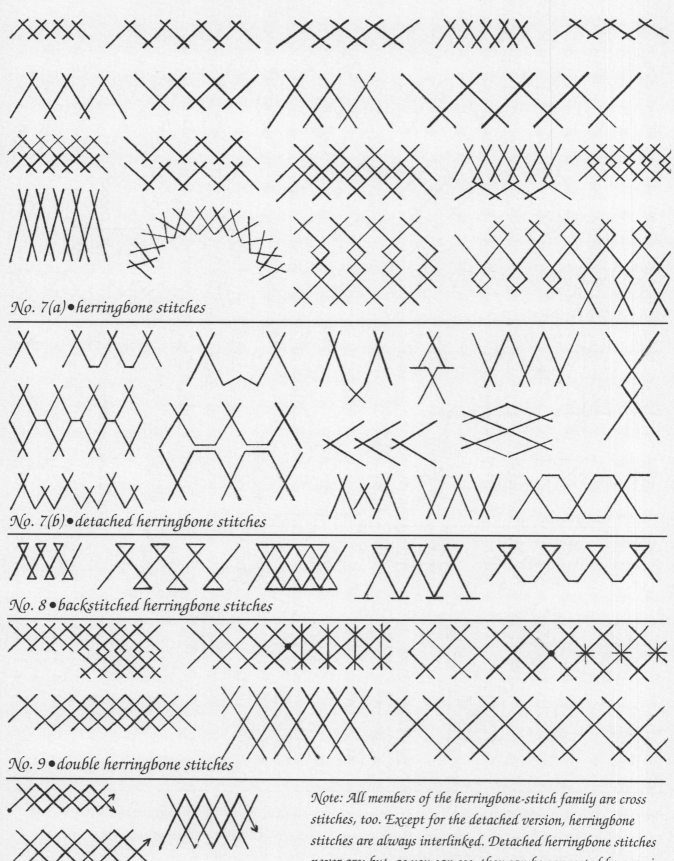

No. 7(a) • herringbone stitches

No. 7(b) • detached herringbone stitches

No. 8 • backstitched herringbone stitches

No. 9 • double herringbone stitches

No. 10 • closed herringbone stitches

Note: All members of the herringbone-stitch family are cross stitches, too. Except for the detached version, herringbone stitches are always interlinked. Detached herringbone stitches never are; but, as you can see, they can be connected by a variety of embellisher stitches.

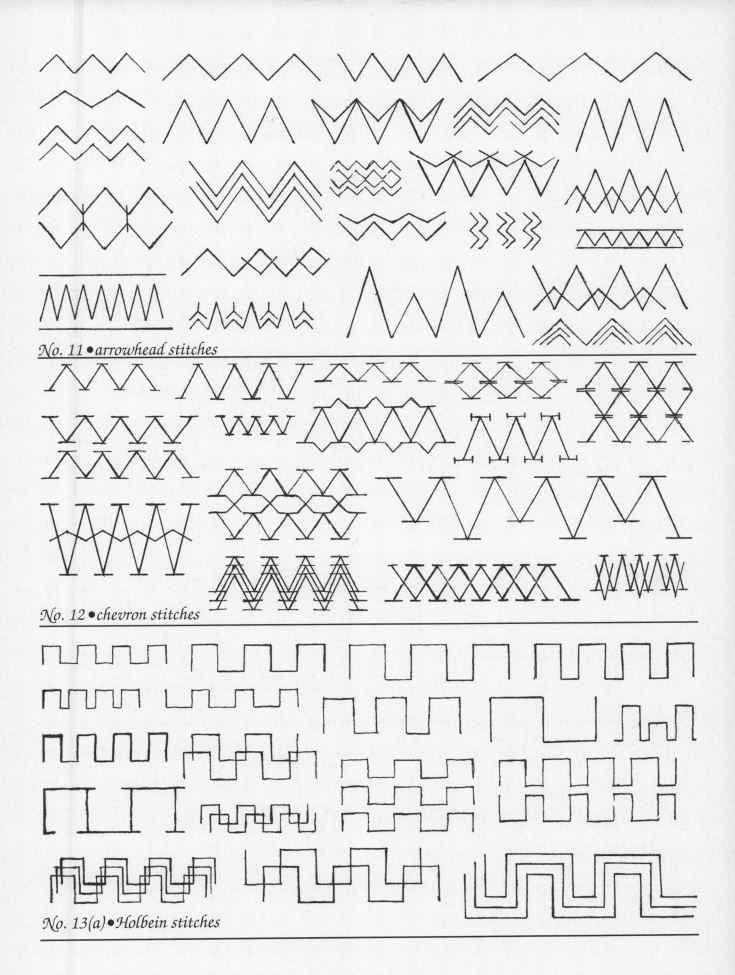

No. 11 • arrowhead stitches

No. 12 • chevron stitches

No. 13(a) • Holbein stitches

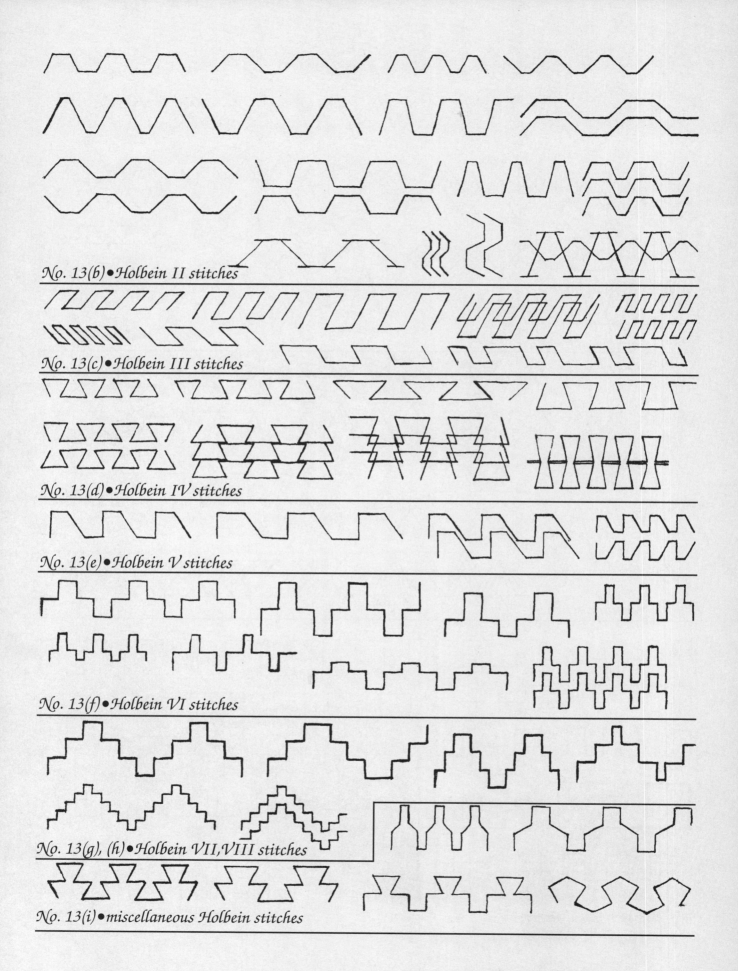

No. 13(b) • *Holbein II stitches*

No. 13(c) • *Holbein III stitches*

No. 13(d) • *Holbein IV stitches*

No. 13(e) • *Holbein V stitches*

No. 13(f) • *Holbein VI stitches*

No. 13(g), (h) • *Holbein VII, VIII stitches*

No. 13(i) • *miscellaneous Holbein stitches*

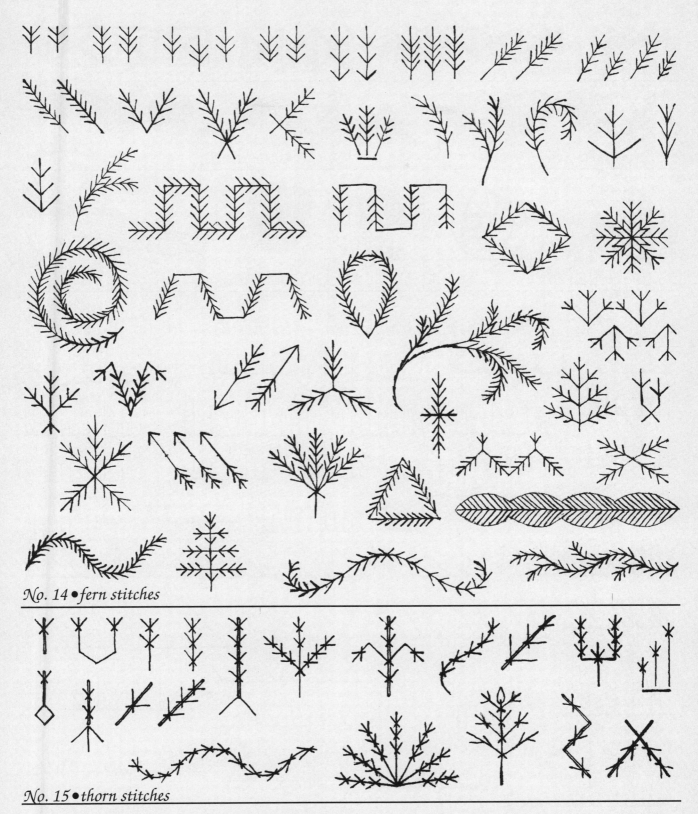

No. 14 • fern stitches

No. 15 • thorn stitches

Note: The generic fern stitch is a specialized backstitch which can be worked along many different lines. Both of the branching stitches in every pair are always directly opposite each other. Thorn stitch combines a laid thread (or several strands) with one or more modified cross stitches which are actually fancy couching stitches. Sometimes the cross stitch legs are also couched to form auxiliary thorn stitches.

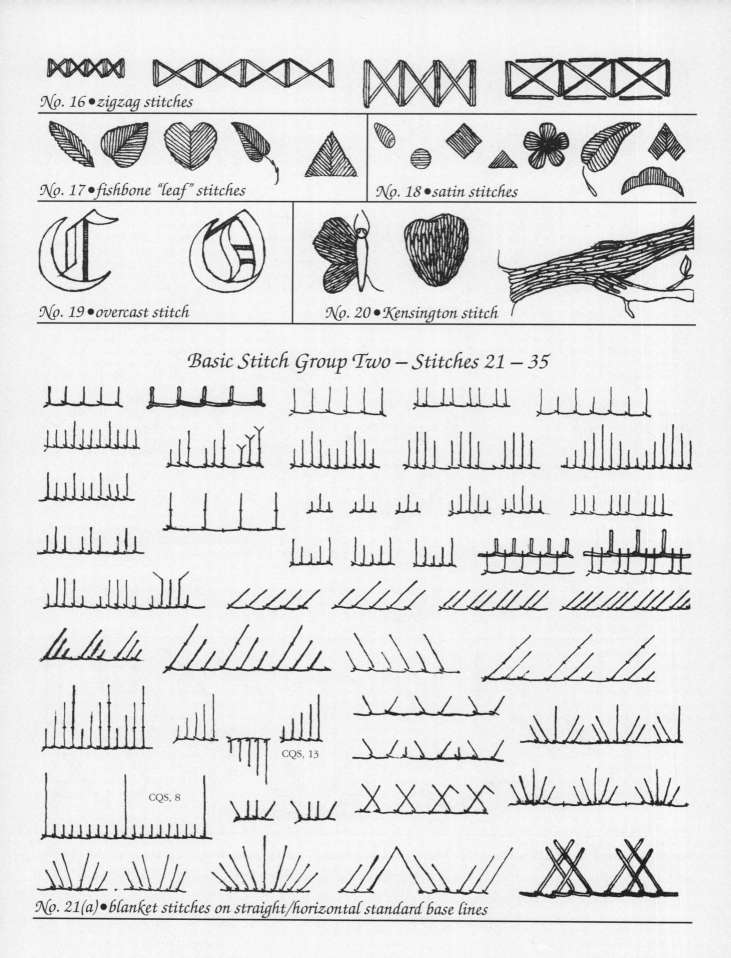

No. 16 • zigzag stitches

No. 17 • fishbone "leaf" stitches

No. 18 • satin stitches

No. 19 • overcast stitch

No. 20 • Kensington stitch

Basic Stitch Group Two – Stitches 21 – 35

CQS, 13

CQS, 8

No. 21(a) • blanket stitches on straight/horizontal standard base lines

Note the necessary couching stitches on several examples. These maintain the curves of the base lines.

No. 21(c)•blanket stitches on "serpentine" standard base lines

No. 21(d)•blanket stitches on "Holbein-stitch" base lines

No. 21(e)•*blanket stitches: "zigzag" and "mock-zigzag" configurations*

No. 21(f)•*blanket stitches: "scalloping" structures*

No. 21(g)•*blanket stitches: circular base lines*

No. 21(h)•*blanket stitches: "free-form" base lines*

No. 21(i)•*"spiraling" blanket stitches*

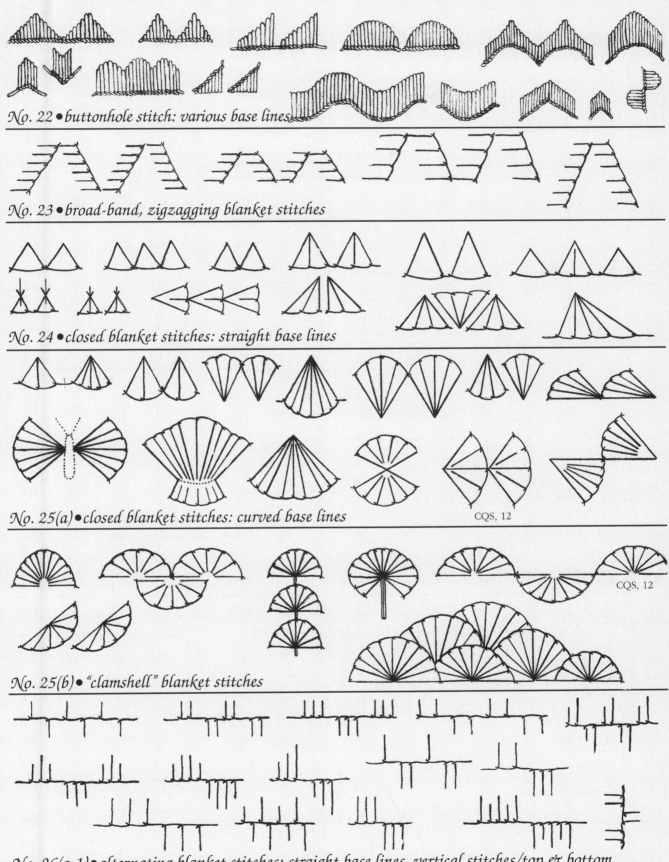

No. 22 • *buttonhole stitch: various base lines*

No. 23 • *broad-band, zigzagging blanket stitches*

No. 24 • *closed blanket stitches: straight base lines*

No. 25(a) • *closed blanket stitches: curved base lines*   CQS, 12

No. 25(b) • *"clamshell" blanket stitches*   CQS, 12

No. 26(a-1) • *alternating blanket stitches: straight base lines, vertical stitches/top & bottom*

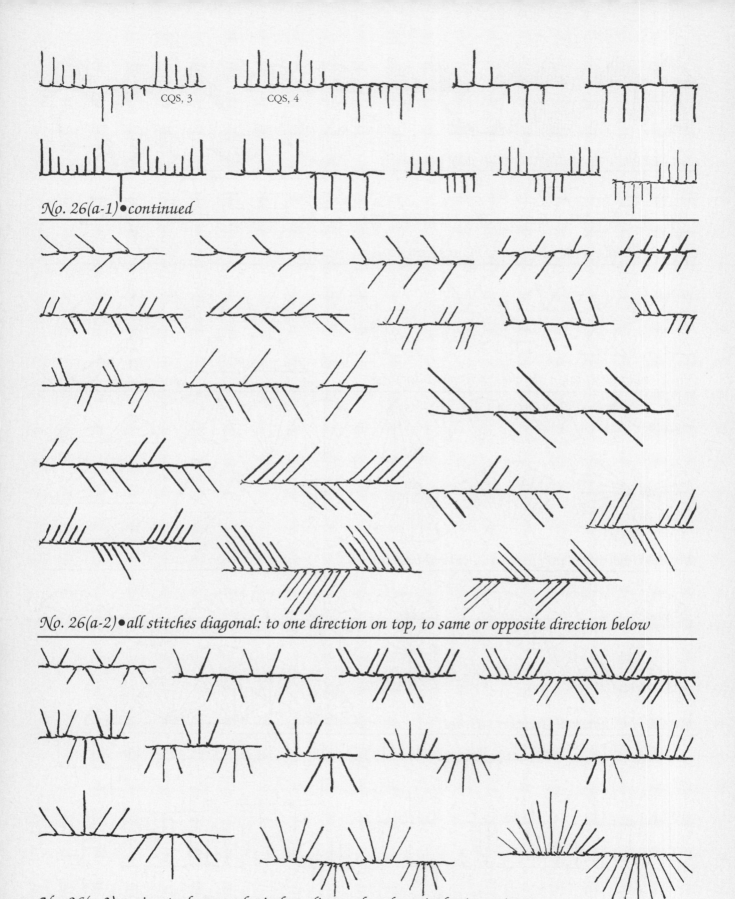

CQS, 3

CQS, 4

No. 26(a-1)•continued

No. 26(a-2)•all stitches diagonal: to one direction on top, to same or opposite direction below

No. 26(a-3)•pairs & clusters of stitches: diagonal and vertical orientations

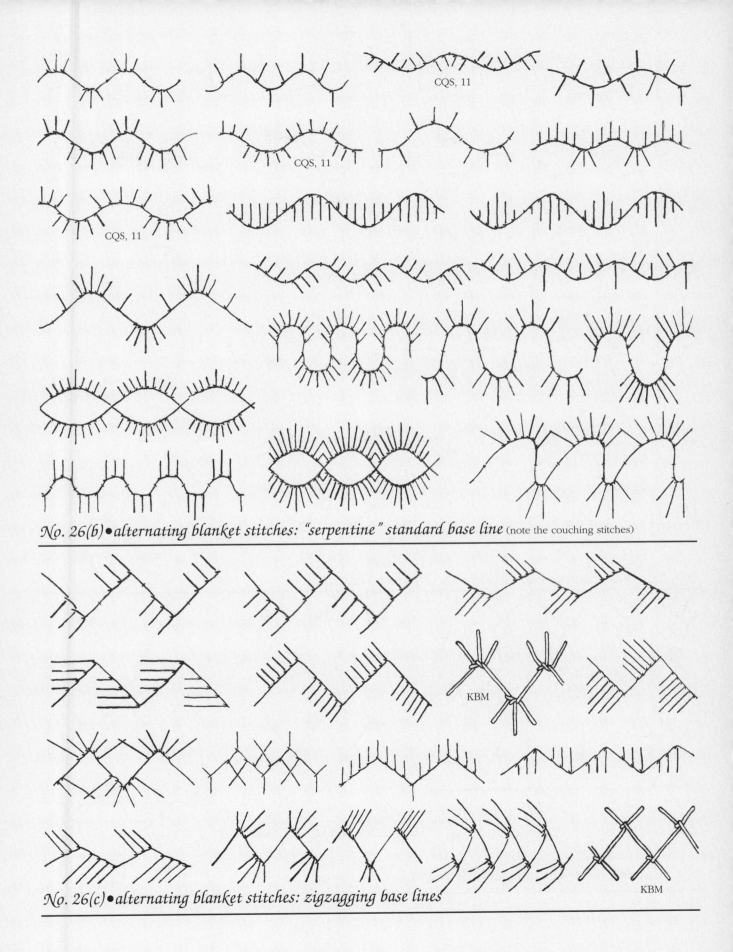

CQS, 11

CQS, 11

CQS, 11

No. 26(b)•alternating blanket stitches: "serpentine" standard base line (note the couching stitches)

KBM

No. 26(c)•alternating blanket stitches: zigzagging base lines

KBM

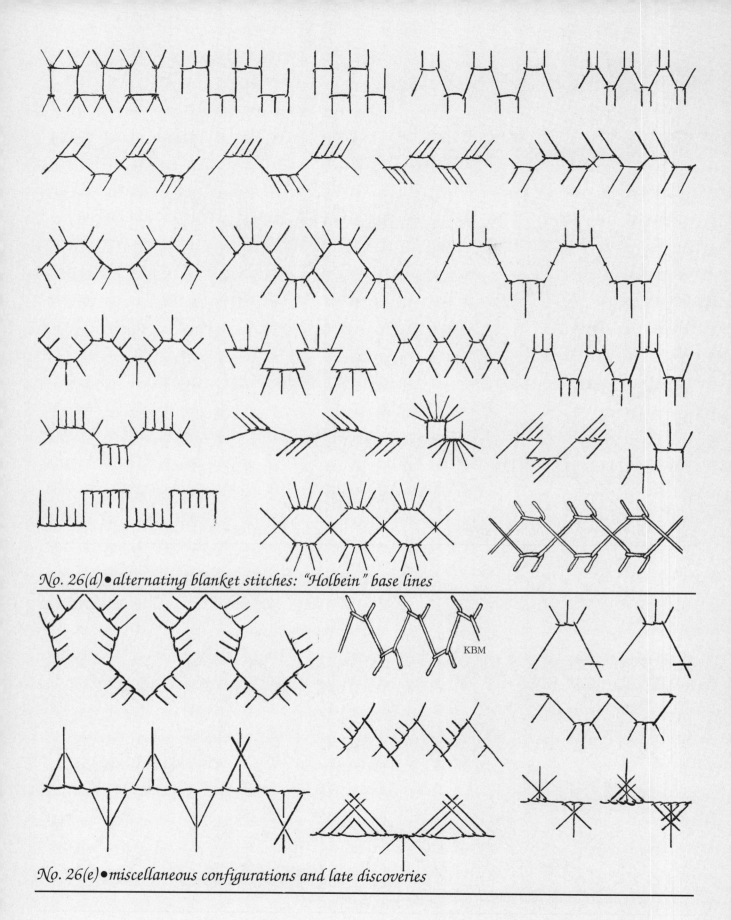

No. 26(d)•alternating blanket stitches: "Holbein" base lines

KBM

No. 26(e)•miscellaneous configurations and late discoveries

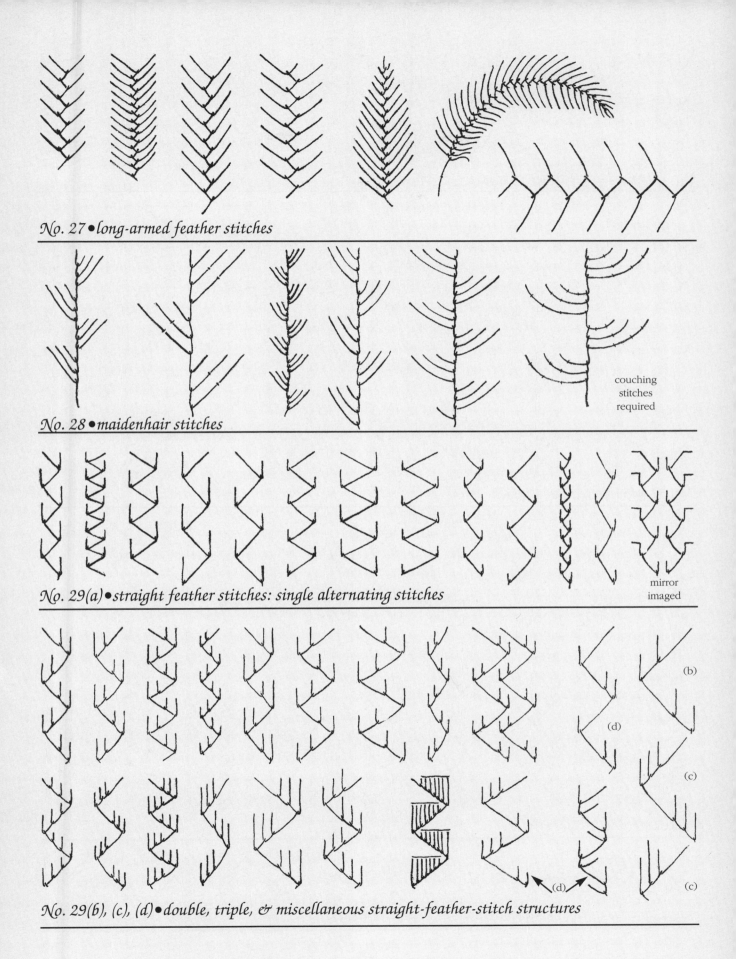

No. 27 • long-armed feather stitches

No. 28 • maidenhair stitches

couching
stitches
required

No. 29(a) • straight feather stitches: single alternating stitches

mirror
imaged

(b)

(d)

(c)

(d)

(c)

No. 29(b), (c), (d) • double, triple, & miscellaneous straight-feather-stitch structures

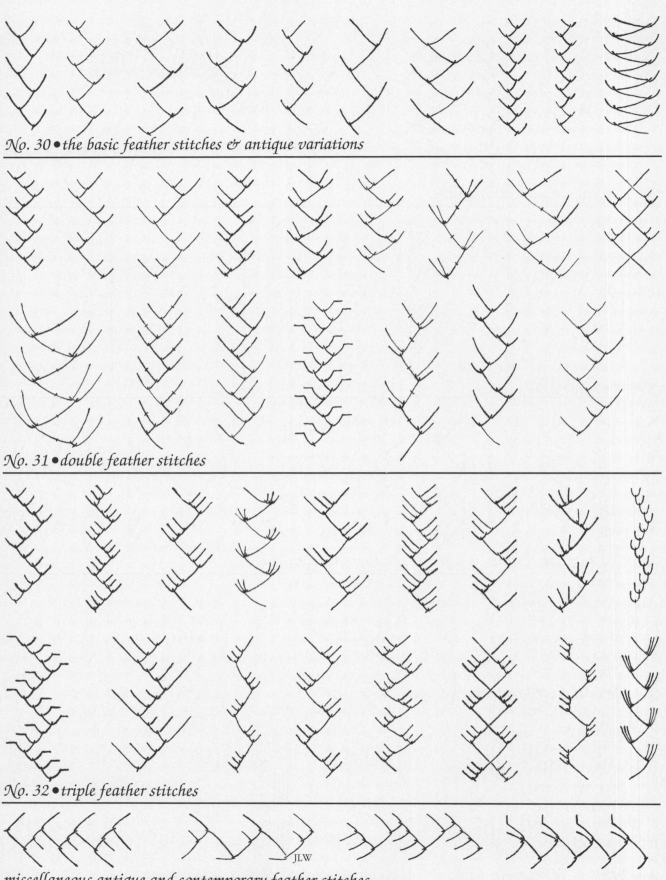

No. 30 • the basic feather stitches & antique variations

No. 31 • double feather stitches

No. 32 • triple feather stitches

JLW

miscellaneous antique and contemporary feather stitches

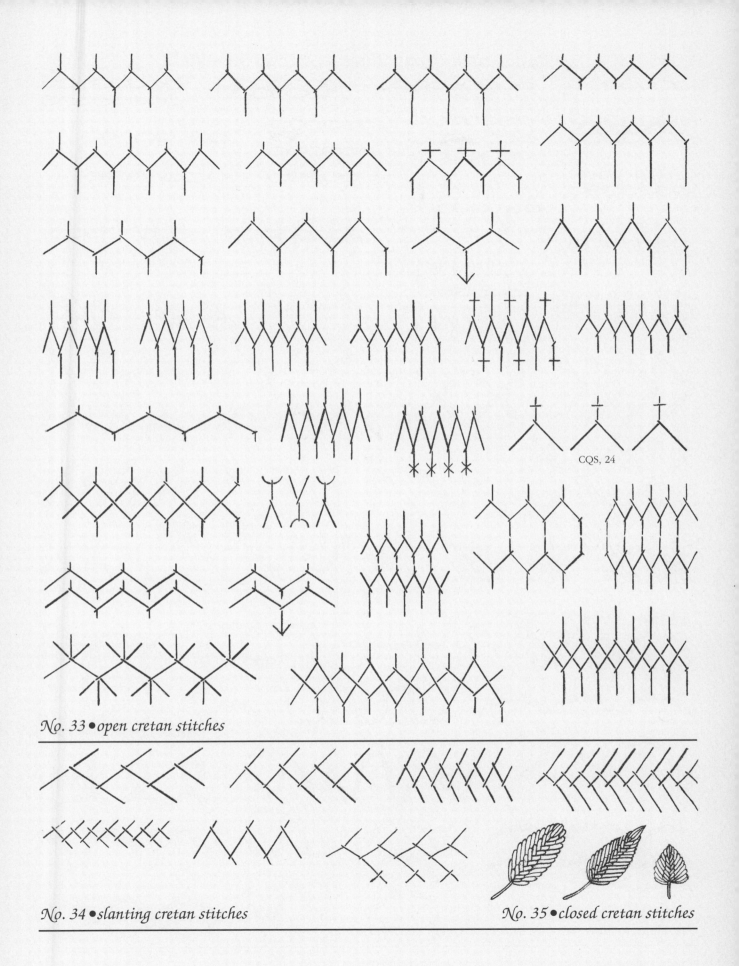

No. 33 • open cretan stitches

No. 34 • slanting cretan stitches

No. 35 • closed cretan stitches

CQS, 24

No. 36(a)•chain stitches: standard linear configurations

---

*No. 38, feathered chain stitch, and No. 40, closed fly stitch, illustrated on p. 133.

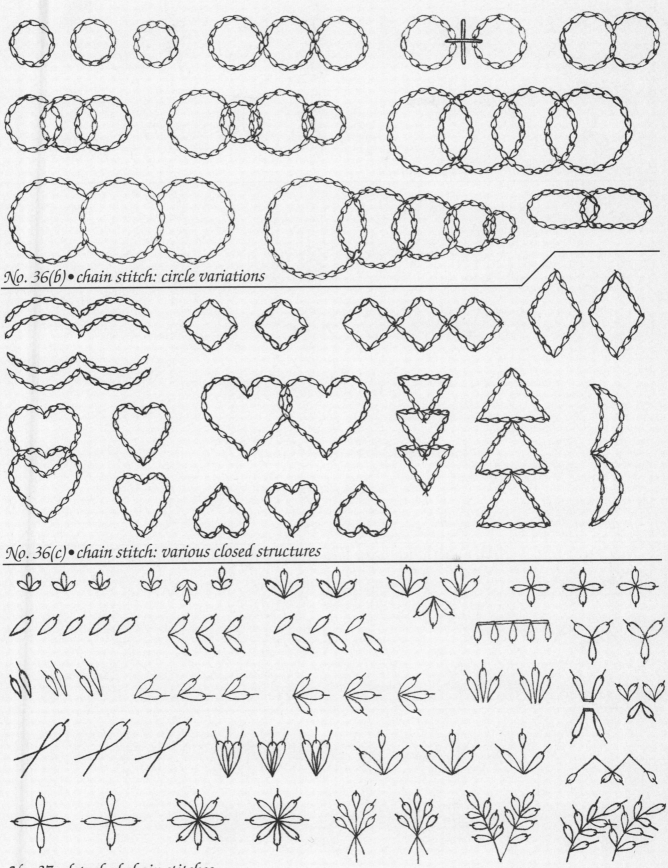

No. 36(b) • *chain stitch: circle variations*

No. 36(c) • *chain stitch: various closed structures*

No. 37 • *detached chain stitches*

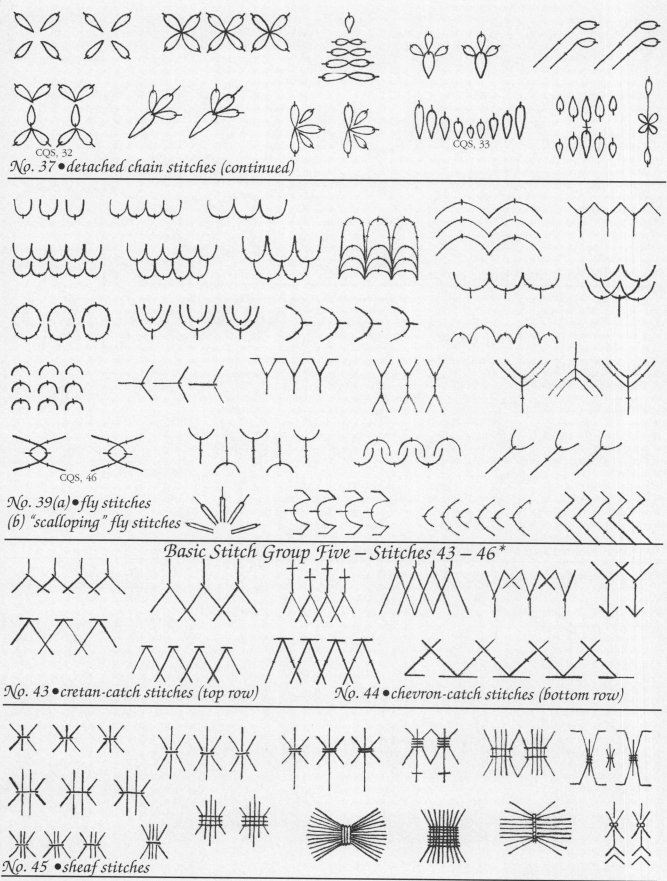

No. 37 • detached chain stitches (continued)

CQS, 32
CQS, 33

No. 39(a) • fly stitches
(b) "scalloping" fly stitches

CQS, 46

Basic Stitch Group Five – Stitches 43 – 46*

No. 43 • cretan-catch stitches (top row)   No. 44 • chevron-catch stitches (bottom row)

No. 45 • sheaf stitches

*No. 46, butterfly chain stitch, illustrated on p. 140.

Basic Stitch Group Four, No. 41, colonial knot, and No. 42, bullion knot, illustrated on p. 137 and p. 159, respectively.

Basic Stitch Group Six, No. 47, interlaced band stitch, and No. 48, laced stepped double-running stitch, illustrated on p. 145.

The Great Pretenders

Have you ever studied a well-focused photograph in a book or magazine and found that, no matter how powerful your magnifying lens, you could not identify the stitch or stitches in the design you were trying to understand? This has happened to me a number of times, and I admit to having been irritated on each occasion, at least partly because I could not draw and, therefore, could not document a particular stitchery until I could decipher it.

Well into the final drafting of the manuscript, I received from Dorothy Bond a 7½ x 8½-inch black-and-white photo of a very elaborately stitched antique crazyquilt that virtually glowed because all of the seamwork embroidery was done in light-colored threads against dark patchwork. Upon close and lengthy inspection, I saw that, with the exception of embellisher knots, four feather-stitch designs, and perhaps a total of ten detached-chain stars on two adjacent seams, all of the primary and embellisher stitches on the entire quilt were from Group One, and there were very few repeats of linear designs. Among the most complex of these, I was surprised to notice several individual primary stitches that nearly fooled me. In fact, for a time, I actually mistook the stars for their regular, straight-stitch variety. What did it all mean?

Once again, I had been given an incredibly important and timely inspiration, and I give all the credit to Mrs. Bond and to my ever-indulgent needlework angel. Although for years I had been aware of the phenomenon — let's call it stitch substitution — I did not realize its significance as a separate crazyquilt-stitchery technique. I began to remember other, simpler examples of stitches that look almost exactly like other stitches, especially Group One stitches posing as stitches from Groups Two and Three. By the end of that happy day, another collaborative effort had produced a page full of look-alike stitches, most of them borrowed from the above-mentioned photograph and from several sheets that Mrs. Bond also sent showing dozens of actual antique stitcheries.

In case you wonder why a substitute might be chosen instead of a regular primary stitch, I can give three reasons. First, at least for some beginning-level embroiderers, straight stitches are often less intimidating and, therefore, are easier to work satisfactorily than blanket and feather stitches. (One noteworthy exception is the comb stitch and its many variations, which I found masquerading as several very intriguing blanket stitches.) Second, each part of a straight-stitch pretender can be worked in a different color and even in a different type of thread, whereas true feather, cretan, blanket, and fly stitches must ordinarily be embroidered with a continuous thread and, thus, in one color (unless, of course, we work with a variegated thread or with two or more different thread colors in the needle at the same time). Third and most importantly, some of the look-alikes permit almost all of the thread to remain on top of the cloth.

The most obvious examples of stitch substitution I found are on the next two pages.

Components of the stitches	Descriptions	Substitute stitch → Primary stitch
	all stitches connect in the middle of the design	
	small stitches connect to the long laid stitch	
	one end of each stitch overlaps	
	both ends of all stitches overlap	
	small stitches connect to the long laid stitch	comb stitches
	short stitches connect ends of longer stitches	
	all stitches connect diagonally along their lengths	
	long and short stitches connect in pairs; alternate orientation	
	stitches connect end to end diagonally and vertically	
	diagonal stitches overlap both ends; add vertical stitches	
	two diagonal stitches connect or overlap at one end; add vertical stitch	
	connect two sets of detached stitches with two or more stacked stitches	
	(note the subtle difference between both primary stitches)	

Treasury of Crazyquilt Stitches…Carole Samples

Components of the stitches	Descriptions	Substitute stitch → Primary stitch
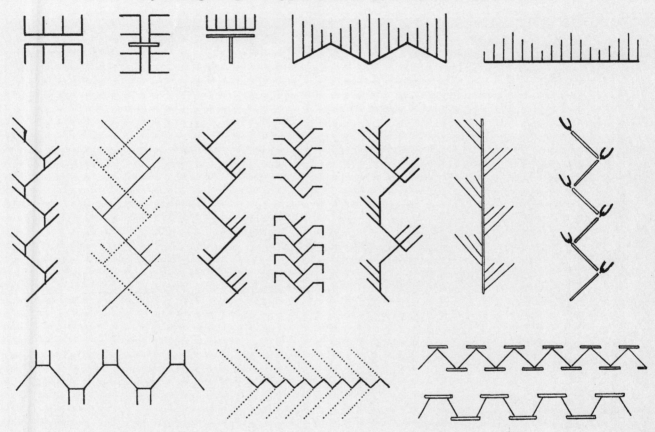	*eight long fly stitches, radiating and equidistant from the center of an imaginary circle and from each other*	

The following antique crazyquilt stitches require no further explanation.

The final look-alike stitch on our list may be the most widely known, although it is impossible to say whether or not it was ever selected by nineteenth-century crazyquilt makers. When worked in one color and in simple continuous lines, either straight, curved, or spiraling, the double running stitch is virtually indistinguishable from the backstitch. Both can be used interchangeably, except the double running stitch (p. 144, Illus. 6-4) can be worked in two alternating colors. In fact, various combinations of threads and colors are possible. You need only imagine how this might be done.

Please record any other examples of similar stitches as soon as you find them. They really are worth searching for!

Chapter Two
Applications

Wool Log Cabin crazyquilt block, Kathy Smith, 1999

" ...But Function Matters, too"
(How to Best Employ the 50 Stitches)

Did you notice the similarities of formation among all of the stitches in each basic stitch group? Let's address the second major aspect of any stitch, that is, how each one can be used on a crazyquilt. Once I realized that there are nine different functions or job descriptions for the 50 stitches we will be using, I created the chart on page 57. It is designed to help you see at a glance as many traditional applications as I could find for each primary and foundation stitch. The following brief descriptions will define and clarify each special function:

1. To outline: These seven stitches are used to "draw" pictures and closed shapes which may or may not be filled in eventually with other stitches (see No. 4 below). The pictures, letters, words, numbers, and musical notations drawn by outlining stitches are usually placed on crazywork patches, borders, or labels rather than on the seams. When used for outlining, the circular and free-form blanket stitches and straight feather stitches generally have to be worked very small to properly render the desired motif.

2. To decorate the seams: With the exception of the Kensington stitch and the overcast stitch, all of the primary stitches can be chosen as the dominant stitch in a linear stitchery. Certain stitches, however, nearly always serve as embellishers. Of all the remaining primary stitches, the bullion knot is least likely to be part of a seamwork design.

3. To decorate the patches: This group includes all of the outlining, filling, leaf-making, and basket-making stitches plus all of the knots, as well as any stitch that might be used for texturing purposes (see pages 209 – 213). The latter are indicated by a capital T on the chart.

4. To fill: Stitches in this category are used to fill an area or portion of a complex design. Some stitches cover an outlined space entirely, as when leaves, flower petals, tree trunks, and the various parts of birds and butterflies, etc., are "painted" in satin, Kensington (long and short satin stitch), stem, or other stitches that are indicated on the chart. A smaller group of stitches can be sprinkled inside a contained shape, thus filling it loosely. (Colonial knots and cross stitches come to mind). By the way, the full-coverage technique is often referred to as "solid filling," while the sprinkling usage is known as "open filling" or "powdering" in professional embroidery circles. A shape need not be outlined first in order to be filled completely with satin, fishbone, closed fly, closed cretan, or Kensington stitches, nor do powdering stitches have to be worked in any sort of regular pattern within the outlined areas they decorate.

5. To appliqué: Eleven of our stitches can attach cloth shapes to the patchwork in a decorative way. The running stitch, though not selected for our master list of primaries, is another suitable choice. Three of the stitches in this group are commonly found in this capacity on antique quilts. The eight that are not traditionally thought of as appliquéing stitches are designated on the chart by the dot in parentheses. I did not indicate every possibility in this category, just the most obvious ones.

6. *To couch:* Many stitches on the list can anchor or fasten not only long or medium-length stitches to prevent their being snagged and broken over time, but some of them are perfect for holding and beautifying plain ribbons and other trims that can be added to the patchwork. Plain couching involves the use of simple, evenly spaced straight stitches, usually tiny enough to be only barely visible, and worked in the same color as the stitches being couched (as, for example, when constructing a spider's web). Any other use of one or more stitches to tie down a thread or a ribbon qualifies as fancy couching. Sometimes the couching stitches must pierce the ribbon (colonial knots, star stitches, and most of the feather stitches, for instance); but usually they form a stitchery "channel" through which the ribbon, trim, or heavier types of thread can be woven. Ordinarily, threads are not pierced by couching stitches.

7. *To tie the quilt:* Isolated stitches and small stitch clusters, when worked through all layers, can also tie a crazyquilt. Use tying stitches along with quilting wherever needed to help support the quilt, placing them at strategic points (not necessarily equidistant from each other) to add yet another decorative element to the blocks.

8. *To finish the edges:* Although I have seen only one crazyquilt with embroidered edges and although only two stitches would traditionally be selected for this purpose, this category is still important to purists and others who love knowing everything about our subject.

9. *To pad a stitch:* As you may have noticed, any motif worked in satin stitches is more beautiful when it or its parts are first embroidered with a preliminary layer of padding stitches. A single underlayer of satin stitches or seed stitches is worked perpendicular to the finish layer of satin stitches, giving the latter a definite dimensional aspect. If two layers of satin stitches, also laid at right angles to each other, are worked underneath the visible, top layer of satin stitches, the technique is known as double padding. It is always best to use padding threads in the same color as the satin stitches on top; but you can choose a less pretentious thread, such as cotton floss, to pad a more expensive fiber, like silk or wool.

Detail from "Sampler Three," by the author, 1995

The Nine Functions of Crazyquilt Stitches

Primary & Preparatory Stitches	Outline	Decorate Seams	Decorate Patches	Fill	Appliqué	Couch	Tie	Finish Edges	Pad
1. straight stitches, various		•	•	•		•	•		
2. backstitch	•	•	•	•	(•)				
3. stem stitch, outline stitch	•	•	•	•					
4. cross/upright-cross stitch		•	•	•	(•)	•	•		
5. star stitches		•	•T	(•)		•	•		
6. snowflake stitches		•	•			•			
7a. herringbone stitch		•	•T	•	(•)	•			
7b. detached herringbone stitch		•	T			•			
8. backstitched herringbone st.		•	T	•		•			
9. double herringbone stitch		•	•T		(•)	•			
10. closed herringbone stitch		•	•T	•		•			
11. arrowhead stitch		•	•T		(•)	•			
12. chevron stitch		•	•T	•		•			
13. Holbein stitches, various		•	•T	•		•			
14. fern stitch		•	•T						
15. thorn stitch		•	•						
16. zigzag stitch		•	(T)			•			
17. fishbone "leaf" stitch		•	•	•					
18. satin stitch		•	•	•	•	(•)		(•)	•
19. overcast stitch			•						
20. Kensington stitch			•	•					
21. blanket stitches, various	g, h	•	some	a,c	•	(•)		•	
22. buttonhole stitch		•			•			•	
23. broad-band zigzag blanket		•				(•)			
24., 25a. closed blanket stitches		•				(•)			
25b. closed blanket stitch var.		•	•T						
26. alternating blanket stitches		•				(•)			
27. long-armed feather stitch		•	•	•		(•)			
28. maidenhair stitch		•				(•)			
29. straight feather stitches	a	•	•T	a		(•)			
30. common feather stitches		•	•T	(•)		a, b			
31. double feather stitches		•	•T			•			
32. triple feather stitches		•	•T			(•)			
33. open cretan stitches		•	T	•		•			
34. slanting cretan stitch		•		•		•			
35. closed cretan stitch		•	•	•					
36. chain stitch	•	•	•T	•	(•)				
37. detached chain stitch		•	•			•	•		
38. "feathered" chain stitch		•				(•)			
39. fly stitch/scalloping fly stitch	•	•	•T		(•)	(•)	•		
40. closed fly stitch		•	•	•					
41. colonial knot		•	•T	•	(•)	•	•		
42. bullion knot		(•)	•						
43. cretan-catch stitch		•				•			
44. chevron-catch stitch		•				•			
45. sheaf stitches, various		•	T	•		•	(•)		
46. butterfly chain stitch		•				•			
47. interlaced band stitch		•	T	(•)		•			
48. laced stepped dbl-running stitch		•	T	(•)		•			
49. split stitch	•			•					
50. seed stitch				•					•

Chapter Three
From Stitch to Stitchery

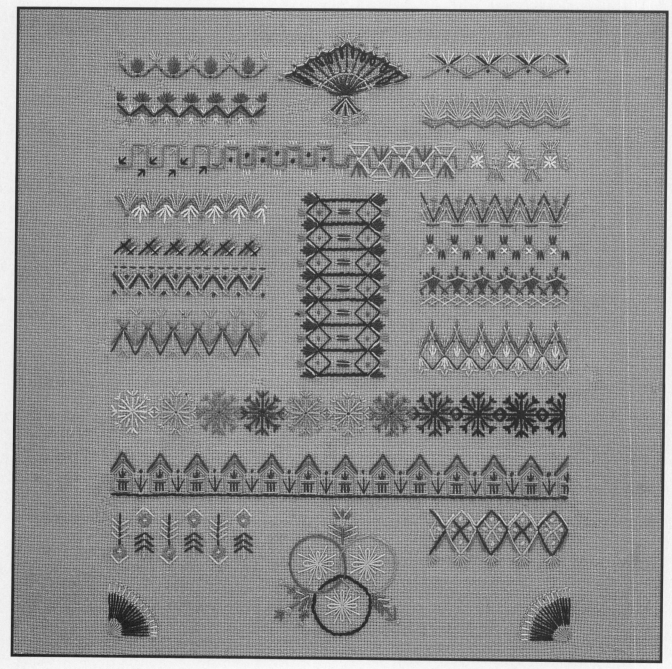

"Sampler Two," by the author, 1992

The Anatomy of a Stitchery: A Few Necessary Terms

In Chapter Three, I will introduce you to the language and design concepts so essential to our understanding of crazyquilt embroidery. Since some of the material will be new to you, and because I sometimes use familiar words in rather unconventional ways, let me begin by defining the most important, crazyquilt-specific terms I will refer to throughout this book. Once you have thoughtfully considered the information on these next few pages, you will be one step closer to learning how every seamwork embroidery design may be visually dissected; and eventually, with practice, you should be able to see how to work even the most intimidating stitch combinations. After all, the ability to embroider anything we want on our crazywork items must surely be one of life's greatest joys!

Here, then, is "A New Vocabulary" for everyone who may be interested in my ideas as well as my stitches:

1. a stitch: After a threaded needle has been pulled through a piece of cloth from the wrong side (WS) until the knot in the thread settles against the cloth, the same needle re-enters the cloth from the top or right side (RS) at some distance from the original exit point, and is pulled with its thread to the WS again, until the thread on top lies neatly, not loosely, on the cloth. One stitch has been formed.

Now, a number of things can happen to that stitch – to the length of thread on top – which define and establish its universal identity (Illus. 3-1). For example: sometimes the working thread on the right side is wound one or more times around the needle before both needle and thread are returned to the wrong side of the cloth (b). These actions form either a knot (colonial or French) or a coil of some length (a bullion knot), each of which is a commonly-known, named stitch.

Completing a stitch might require the working thread to "engage" the partially-formed stitch in such a way that it bends sharply (c). Or, the needle and working thread, on each subsequent return to the RS after the first stitch is made, can pierce the thread at short intervals along its length, creating a chain of split stitches (d). Or, the first stitch made on the RS can be formed into a loop or teardrop and held in place with the help of your freehand thumb while the next action of the needle and thread creates a tie stitch which permanently fastens the loop to the RS of the cloth. This thread formation is formally known as a detached chain stitch and is shown with other curved stitches (e) and (f).

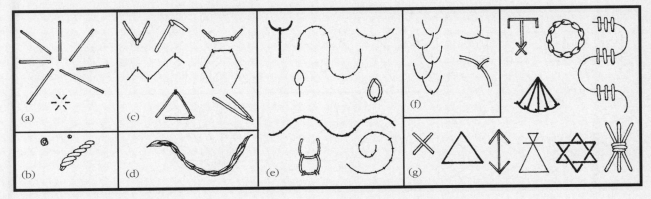

Illus. 3-1

As you can see, the curved stitches require the addition of plain couching stitches to hold every short curve and long, serpentine or spiraling thread in place. Please note, too, that the tie stitches which fasten fly stitches and detached chains may be so small that they are barely discernible; but we can make them as long as we wish — even bending or curving them, if we like.

Last of all the thread manipulations, I selected a few compound stitches to show you. Each of these is made with two or more separate, complete stitches (not counting couching stitches) as defined on the preceding page, and together form one recognizable, repeatable motif (g). Thus, ...

2. ... a stitch is also any combination of needle-and-thread actions on cloth or other materials which is understood to compose one distinct unit of needlework in thread, yarn, or even beads, and to which a name might be given. For our purposes, Illus. 3-1 provides a good sampling of eleven standard stitch formats, including the bundled example (a sheaf-stitch variation) and the woven-thread configuration in (g). These are the most basic creative "interventions" a needle artist can make whenever she takes up free-style/surface embroidery. From these simple operations, thousands of possible crazyquilt stitches have been and will be invented, and from those stitches, our gorgeous stitcheries are born.

3. a stitchery (plural, stitcheries): a decorative embroidery design, that is to say, the entire group of stitches which together form one stitched decoration for the seams and patches of crazyquilts. (The individually-worked designs on my samplers are also called stitcheries.) There are five essential types of stitcheries to be found on nineteenth-century crazyquilts: linear, embellisher, "patch picture," writing, and texturing. Please consider the following:

4. a linear or seamwork stitchery: One stitch or stitch cluster can be repeated enough times to cover or otherwise decorate the seam between two pieces of cloth. Except for a very few "spot motifs" which somehow made their way onto the pages, all of the designs in Chapters One through Six in Part Two are intended for patchwork seams.

According to our definition, then, a linear stitchery may consist of one entire stitch, named or not, single or compound, worked several times in a row, using the same thread and color for all of the stitches, and having no other stitches added for adornment, as seen below in Illus. 3-2 (a). Ordinarily, however, the chosen primary stitches will all be deco-

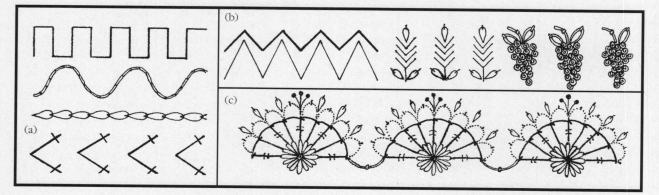

Illus. 3-2

rated with at least one additional, subordinate stitch; and very often those extra stitches were combined into wonderfully complex units of design which I call embellishers. The previous graphic shows the range of possibilities from simple, one-element designs (a) to a very elaborate, five- or six-element linear stitchery (c).

Every seamwork stitchery has two generic placement options relative to the seam that it decorates: (a) it can straddle the seam, in which case the needlework design will either be centered upon the seam, or worked with more than half its width to one side of the seam and the remainder of its width on the opposite side; or (b) the stitchery can be positioned entirely to one side of its seam, either barely touching it or not touching it at all. If the latter option is chosen, the same stitchery can be used to decorate all the edges of its patch, or various linear designs could be worked along the edges of one patch, one stitchery per edge. Illus. 3-3 has examples of every option described here.

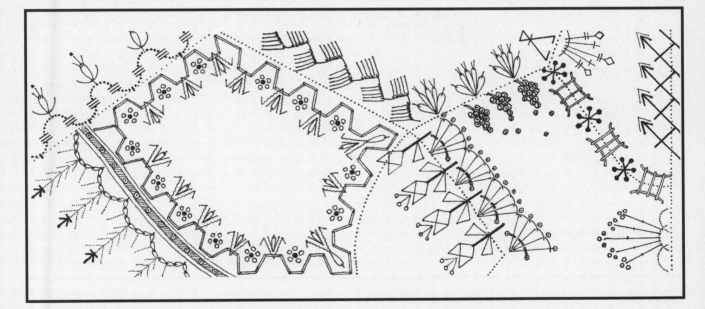

Illus. 3-3

It should also be noted that linear designs were occasionally used "off seam," that is to say, several antique crazyquilts which I have seen contain a number of alternative uses for this type of stitchery. Traditional applications include the decoration of a quilt's border, a length of ribbon, or even a wide binding with a linear design. Another ingenious idea was to embroider a linear stitchery across a patch, from one edge to its opposite edge, thus visually converting one patch into two. This was especially effective when the piece of cloth was larger than other patches in the block or whole-cloth quilt being made. Much more information on specific linear activity will be offered in the next chapter.

5. a primary stitch (plural, primaries): In 99.9 percent of all cases, the primary stitches in any stitchery are worked first. Additionally, from this page forward, this term shall mean "the most important stitch in a stitchery." A stitch will usually be considered the dominant one based upon its noticeability, either by virtue of its greater size, by the type and/or thickness of the thread (or by the greater number of strands used, if applic-

able), or perhaps by the color of the thread which forms the stitch. Very seldom will it be difficult to determine which of the stitches in a complex stitchery is primary, even when it is not the largest component of the entire design.

Primary stitches come in four standard configurations, shown below:
(a) connected/continuous, in which all of the repeated stitches touch along the line without crossing over each other; (b) linked, in which the stitches naturally interconnect (as do herringbone, feather, blanket, and chain stitches); (c) detached, with a space between each stitch repetition; and (d) stacked/multiples, in which any stitch can be worked two or more times very near one another, in a staggered setting or an "echoing" formation, or in any original pattern of repetition. Traditionally, each row of a primary stitch was worked in just one color throughout the entire stitchery.

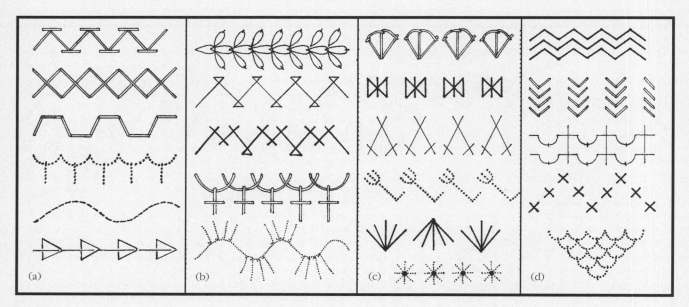

Illus. 3-4

6. an embellisher: Many single stitches and combinations of stitches can be embroidered on or very close to the primary stitches in a complex stitchery. (In fact, by definition, every multi-stitch embellisher is a specialized stitchery.) They do what their name implies: they make other stitches — the primary stitches in linear and texturing designs — as well as whole alphabet letters fancier, more elaborate-looking, more beautiful.

In Part Two, Chapter Seven, I have described the six special-use embellishers along with more than 19 placement possibilities (pages 147 – 151). Whenever the primary stitches in a complex linear design are decorated with two or more embellishers, one of those will most likely be dominant, appearing to be the most essential stitch or stitch cluster used to complete the entire stitchery. Subordinate embellishers in the same design will obviously be less important to the final result. As you collect and document antique-crazyquilt stitcheries, you will see that subordinate embellishers such as colonial/French knots, little cross stitches, or radiating straight stitches to name just a few, often decorate embellishers which are visually dominant.

Embellishers of either status may be worked in any size required, even larger than the primary stitches they decorate, and are often more complex than their primaries. Except when non-traditional effects are sought, every different embellisher in a stitchery should be worked in its own color or color combination; and the embellishers' colors must not be the same as that of the primary stitch which they adorn.

7. a stitch cluster: Another special needlework device for crazyquilts was created by combining two or more stitches in a pleasing formation. These stitcheries, which can be worked in any desirable size and which could be composed of as many as 30 to 35 individual, simple, or compound stitches, always contain a dominant stitch that is repeated at least once. Most of the clusters we might either find on old quilts or invent for ourselves — and there are literally thousands of possible combinations — can be used as embellishers in some linear designs and as the primary stitches in others. Additionally, a suitably-sized, non-repeating stitch cluster can serve as a spot motif on a patch, while texturing patterns are sometimes created by scattering or uniformly repeating one or more clusters all over a patch (see Chapter Twelve in Part Two).

Shown here are 24 examples of authentic antique-quilt designs, and one extra cluster, the grapes, which are truly representative of the best stitcheries in this category:

Illus. 3-5

8. "patch pictures" and spot motifs: As we all know, the nineteenth-century needle artists who made crazyquilts were not content to merely embroider on the seams of their patchwork; they often added a wonderful decorative element to the visual feast by stitching (or painting) certain recognizable objects and other non-figurative designs upon patches which usually contained the designs entirely. (Very infrequently, however, one of these stitcheries was allowed to spill over onto an adjacent patch or two.)

Whether realistic, cartoon-like, or purely ornamental, every patch picture we can discover and document gives us evidence of the things which were most aesthetically desirable and of material importance to women of that time. The following list of stitchable images is pretty much exhaustive, covering every traditional type known to me as well as a number of contemporary references. More than 260 animate and inanimate subjects, "doodle-stitch" pictures, and three kinds of spot motifs (including my own little fans and hearts) can be found on pages 163 – 197. These include:

   (a) representational/figurative/pictorial designs
      1. human figures, whole or partial, including Kate Greenaway's children, storybook characters, historical and mythological persons, and mermaids
      2. angels (not common), especially, a head with wings beneath or surrounding it
      3. animals (warm- and cold-blooded) and fish

4. birds, especially owls, cranes, swallows, and peacocks

5. butterflies and moths (realistic and fantasy creatures)

6. insects and spiders (ditto)

7. realistic floral and plant life, trees, ferns; a bouquet in the hand; thistles and `
	shamrocks; fruit

8. household items, kitchenware: ewer-and-basin, lamps, butter churn, coffee
	mill, silverware, old kettles, jars; vases and baskets to hold flowers or fruit

9. sewing tools and machines; other needlework paraphernalia

10. ladies' and men's wearing apparel and accessory items: bonnets, boots, gloves,
	comb and brush, bamboo fans, umbrellas; pocket watch; crowns

11. food items and their containers

12. decorative porcelain and china pieces: large floor urns, tea pots, cups and
	saucers, flower pots, painted dinner plates

13. buildings, bridges, fences, and other useful structures; windmills, lighthouses

14. scenic landscapes (often painted on porcelain items)

15. musical instruments

16. religious symbols and articles

17. patriotic symbols and flags

18. organizational and fraternal insignia

19. toys

20. horseshoes (with or without floral decoration)

21. tools (all professions and trades)

22. sporting equipment: canoe, oars, rifle, bow and arrow, saddle

23. home furnishings and appliances: ladder-back chair, tall case clocks and
	mantle clocks, rocking chairs, old wringer washer; a Victrola

24. vehicles of every kind (land-, air-, and water-worthy); baby buggy, bicycles,
	hot-air balloons

25. weapons: old cannon, rifle/shotgun/muzzle-loader, pistol; swords

26. spiders' webs   27. birds' nests with eggs   28. shaving mug and razor

(b) non-representational designs — the stylized drawings which depict in a less realistic manner things which exist in life or in our imaginations, such as:

1. simple or fantasy flowers/bouquets, trees, and sprigs; underwater plant life

2. a sun, moon, stars, and clouds in cartoon mode

3. comets

4. a musical notation, including treble clef, staff, and notes (see Crazy Quilts,
	pages 34 – 35)

5. interlocking rings (two or more in a straight row; three or five in a circular
	formation)

6. "roundels" and medallion-style designs shaped as ovals, squares, rectangles,
	and "diamonds" (page 183)

7. "frames" and cartouches (open in their centers and large enough to contain an
	initial, a monogram, or other design)

8. *little fan stitcheries*
9. *hearts/Valentine motifs*
10. *single paisley spot motifs*
11. *"Blue Willow" land/seascapes*

(c) contemporary design possibilities, mythical and late-twentieth-century and new-millenium images that were not stitched on antique crazyquilts:

1. *fairies, elves, leprechauns, wood sprites, and their kinfolk*
2. *mythical and prehistoric creatures: dragons, dinosaurs; "Nessie"*
3. *comic-book/comic-strip/coloring-book and animated-feature-film and television series characters (use only with permission in writing from the creators or film studios)*
4. *Santas of all kinds*
5. *complex "adult angel" figures, head-to-toe renderings; many hold some object in their hands*
6. *artifacts and structures relating to Native American, Egyptian, Celtic, Samurai, Maori, Old Roman, and other cultures*
7. *future-world objects, vehicles, and persons in the popular literature of our day, such as a Star Trek "com" badge, Dr. Who's T.A.R.D.I.S., Star Wars characters, etc. (again, use only with permission)*
8. *electric-powered and digital work savers, including office equipment: computer with monitor, lap-top version, mouse; cell phones, beepers, satellite dish, and the like*
9. *fitness and sporting equipment and vehicles: golf bag, skateboard, power boat, hand weights, roller blades, etc.*
10. *modern-day athletic figures: joggers, skiers, golfers, figure skater, football player, scuba diver, martial artist*
11. *anyone and anything related to dance, all forms*
12. *thatch-roofed cottages*
13. *medieval and Renaissance-era objects and persons; also, anything reminiscent of Camelot, King Arthur, Queen Guinevere, et al.*
14. *cattle brands*
15. *farm/ranch equipment*
16. *modern-day toys, dolls*
17. *vintage automobiles (I have never seen one on an old quilt, and I cannot imagine why)*

Isn't this wonderful? And fun! It has to be obvious to you that any item or individual that interests you can be and should be stitched upon patches in your crazywork. These are but a few suggestions from my own "database" of graphic illustrations, photos, and tracings of the things I hope to use one day. My public librarians, by the way, have always graciously helped me find every business and museum address I ever needed when seeking permission to include someone else's creations in my work. With so many sources and with our imaginations fully on, we will have enough patch-picture material for another century!

Chapter Four
The Art of Linear Stitchery

Crazyquilt block, by the author, 1993

Multiples and Modifications

As we come to the final pages in Part One of *Treasury of Crazyquilt Stitches*, there must be many of my readers who are marveling at all of the technical aspects pertaining to crazyquilt embroidery. I promised myself that I would share as many of my intriguing observations on the subject as available space would allow. Only three more very important design concepts remain before we proceed to the collections of seamwork stitcheries from my own imagination and others from quilts of long ago.

With your permission, I would begin by borrowing the format of Chapter Three, thus defining two additional terms needed by everyone who wants to create original linear designs. To continue from page 65:

9. the orientation of a stitch is its direction relative to its patchwork seam when repeated in a straight line along that seam. In other words, the primary stitches (and embellishers) in a linear stitchery are very often, but not always, directional, possessing an "up" and a "down" – or a "top" and a "bottom" – inherent to their structures. Or, instead of being worked in true vertical modes, stitches might be given diagonal-left or diagonal-right orientation; they might be worked above or below the seam. And, of course, the same stitch (simple or compound) can be clustered, in which case the orientation is multi-directional.

You will most likely find directional stitches among those in Basic Stitch Groups One, Two, and Three; however, only certain stitches in each category can be made to work in diagonal confiurations. The following examples of each directional possibility are accompanied by a small arrow, "to help you see what I see when I dissect a stitchery."

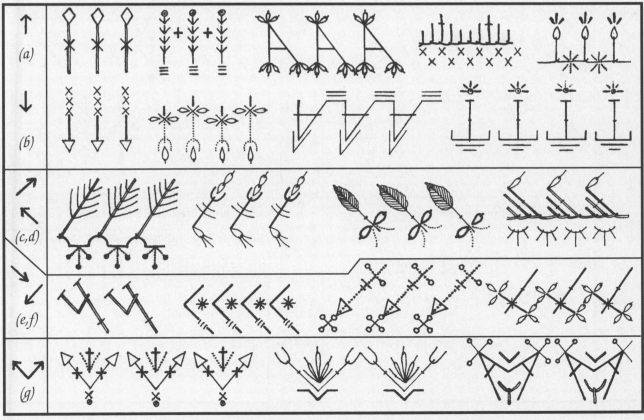

Illus. 4-1

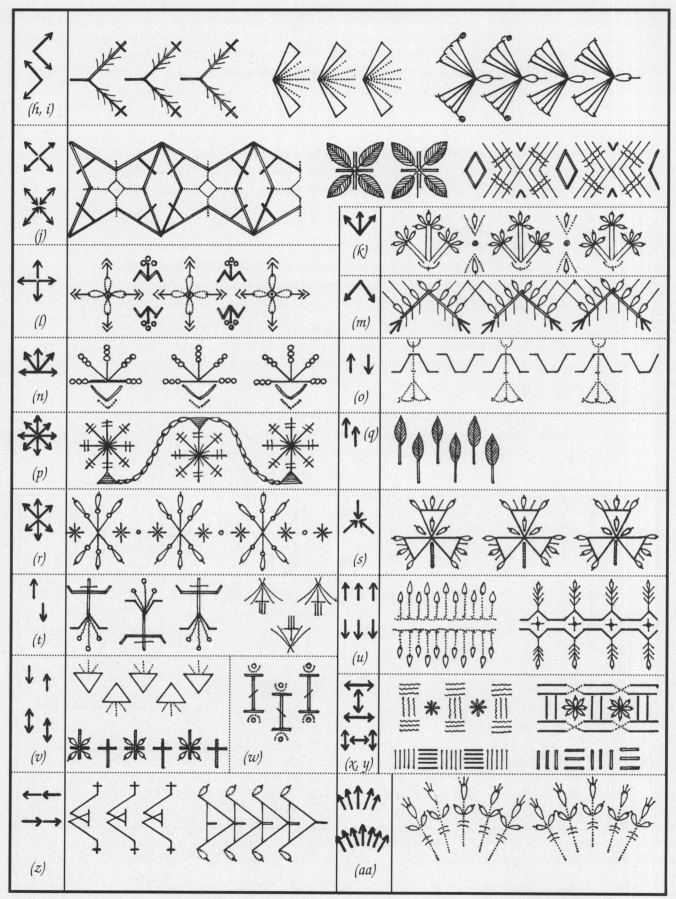

Illus. 4-1, continued

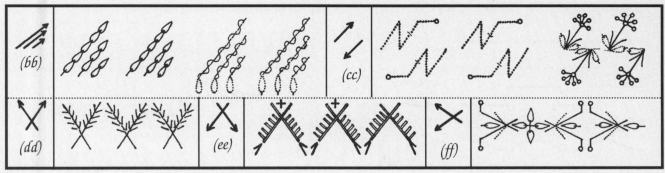

Illus. 4-1, continued

The first thirty-two modes of orientation for individual primary stitches are the most commonly found of all the directionals, but they are just the beginning! Illus. 4-2(a) has nine configurative diagrams which represent several less familiar but nonetheless traditional stitches while (b) contains guidelines only for stitches which may be superimposed upon one another rather than more ideas relative to stitch orientation. Please consult the Dictionary for examples of actual stitches which conform to these structures.

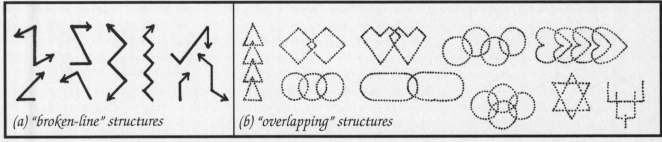

(a) "broken-line" structures   (b) "overlapping" structures

Illus. 4-2

One of my best discoveries of all time is the next concept in our study:

10. the standard stitchery base lines, or SBLs. The primary stitches in a linear design, in addition to being worked in a straight line, can be made to follow a variety of "pathways" along a seam (or upon a patch). Most of these stitchery base lines have been standardized by many years of use. The most commonly chosen SBLs are shown in Illus. 4-3, with several sample stitcheries in accompaniment.

I must tell you that not every primary stitch can follow every stitchery base line. If you have any doubt about whether or not a particular stitch will work along a chosen SBL, by all means draw your stitchery on cross section paper first. Otherwise, you have all of the designs in the next six chapters to inspire you!

One further note: although we almost always see continuous linear designs on old crazyquilts (with the primary stitches repeated in an unbroken line along the seam they decorate), stitchery base lines can also follow an interrupted path, with significant spaces between groups of two or more primaries. The diagrams and designs on page 70 focus entirely on single-row stitcheries. Wait until you see how many things you can do with several repeating rows of the same primary stitch!

The final group of illustrations reveals several of my remaining findings on the subject of special seamwork-stitchery possibilities. I hope the graphics will be self-explanatory and helpful to those of you who intend to design linear combinations.

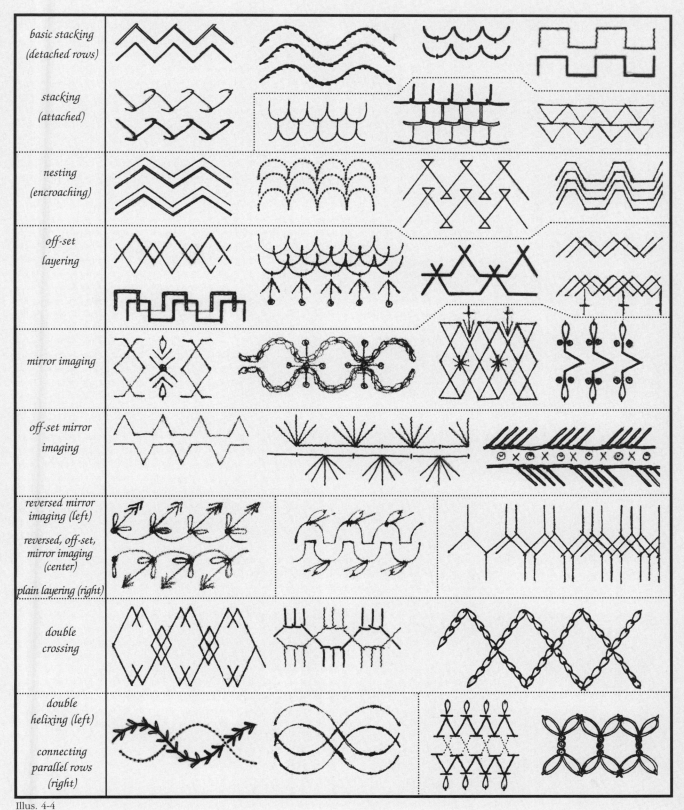

The following table accompanies the illustration:

basic stacking (detached rows)	
stacking (attached)	
nesting (encroaching)	
off-set layering	
mirror imaging	
off-set mirror imaging	
reversed mirror imaging (left) / reversed, off-set, mirror imaging (center) / plain layering (right)	
double crossing	
double helixing (left) / connecting parallel rows (right)	

Part Two

The
Stitcheries

Crazyquilt block, Lynn E. Tolles, 1998

Chapter One
Straight-Thread-Stitch Designs

Pretty Patches Under Glass, by the author, 1992

A very versatile, very valuable stitch
or the most variable stitch of all

We might call them in-and-out stitches, or more appropriately perhaps, out-and-in stitches. A straight stitch is what happens when the needle and thread exit the cloth at one point on top of the work, and are then returned to the back of the work at some distance from that point of origin, with the working thread eventually pulled tight against the cloth on top. This definition is deceptively simple, however, as the following pages will prove.

In fact, I have just described a common or generic straight stitch, sometimes referred to as the flat stitch. There are literally thousands of possible variations that belong to Basic Stitch Group One. These can be made in any practical length and can lie in any direction. To visualize the latter possibilities, think of a circle drafted on paper with all 360 of its radii represented.

There is one defining element with regard to straight stitches that is almost too obvious to mention, but I am going to do so anyway. Straight stitches are always straight! Unlike any of the stitches from the other five basic stitch groups, the same needle and thread which have made a straight stitch and which remain connected to it may never act upon that stitch in a way that causes it to bend or twist. Having said that, there are, of course, times when it is desirable, even necessary, to bend a straight stitch. Sheaf stitches and certain spiders' webs are very important exceptions to the no-bend rule. If you must bend or curve a stitch that starts out straight, it is permissible to use a separate thread to couch or fasten it in place.

The named stitches in Group One are numbered from one through 20; but as previously stated, 16 of those are actually "umbrella groups," each composed of several stitches that are similar in appearance and formation. The 20 stitches thus become many hundreds, especially when all of stitch No. 1's named and unnamed variations are counted.

Among the seamwork stitches I have documented from all six groups over the years were many that did not have names. I knew they were important, but I didn't know what to do with them. Only one book, Crazy Quilt Stitches, features linear stitcheries that are also based on these anonymous stitches; and it was the chapter on "Kindred Stitches" that finally put them all in perspective. At last I understood the several structural similarities by which these genuine antique-quilt stitches which were never included in standard books on hand embroidery could be organized.

Eventually, by studying many antique crazyquilts and drawing their individual seamwork stitcheries, it became clear that every straight stitch on my list except the overcast and Kensington stitch has multiple versions or possible configurations. Even the lowly backstitch, seldom used to decorate seams, the fern stitch, and the cross stitch have various authentic forms which were selected over and over again by crazyquilt makers long ago. Very often, compound primary stitches were worked all in one color, without embellishers of any kind. The very simplest of the No. 1 stitches were also the best choices

for mirror imaging, and doubling them in this way made their stitcheries appear to be more interesting. I did not design many of these for this book, but they should not be overlooked.

Those of you who examine antique crazyquilts with particular attention to the seamwork embroidery know that five of the primary stitches on our master list are rarely, if ever, used in linear mode on the patchwork seams. The overcast stitch, already mentioned, is one of the handful of stitches with very narrowly defined job descriptions. In this case, it is often paired with the satin stitch to complete the straight bars and curved flourishes on both Gothic-style and script-style lettering. Likewise, the fishbone "leaf" stitch and the stem-stitch rose — two of the three strictly contemporary stitches among the 48 primaries — are far more likely to be employed as embellishers in a seamwork design today; I have never seen either stitch on an antique quilt.

As for the Kensington stitch, its traditional purpose was to render the very beautiful and realistic-looking figurative motifs referred to as patch pictures in this book. "Thread painting" in Kensington stitch was the means by which advanced-level needle artists could create birds and butterflies and floral designs that might seem ready to fly off the quilt or to grow upon it, respectively. The other solid-filling stitch chosen for this same purpose was useful when the area to be filled in was small, perhaps no more than ⅜ inch in width. Few satin-stitch-based seamwork designs are found on antique quilts, however. Whereas I have intentionally given them status as the primary stitches in each of my designs on page 101, satin stitches usually decorated other linear stitches on antique quilts.

The third modern stitch for linear application to make the master list is the zigzag stitch. It is one of the basic band or border stitches and looks somewhat like a fence one might see along a country road. I tried for two years to locate a zigzag stitch design on an old crazyquilt, without any luck. Just as I had nearly given up the hunt for a stitchery based on the backstitched herringbone stitch, I found one in a photograph of an antique quilt. Both stitches will challenge most crazyquilters to a certain extent, but they are well worth the extra effort required.

All told, Chapter One contains no fewer than 900 stitcheries which I designed for seamwork embellishment, although certainly not all of them can be considered original. Somehow, 11 spot motifs made their way onto these pages early on, and I decided to leave them here rather than transfer them to Chapter Eight where they more appropriately belong. Finally, the six pages of authentic stitch combinations representing 18 to 20 antique quilts, pgs. 104 – 109, were selected from my own personal registry of old linear designs. At least a small number of these may surprise and delight you with their complexity or eccentricity, while others are quite ordinary. Here is the greatest proof, if you need any, of the incredible artistic variety available to us within this first category of hand-embroidery stitches.

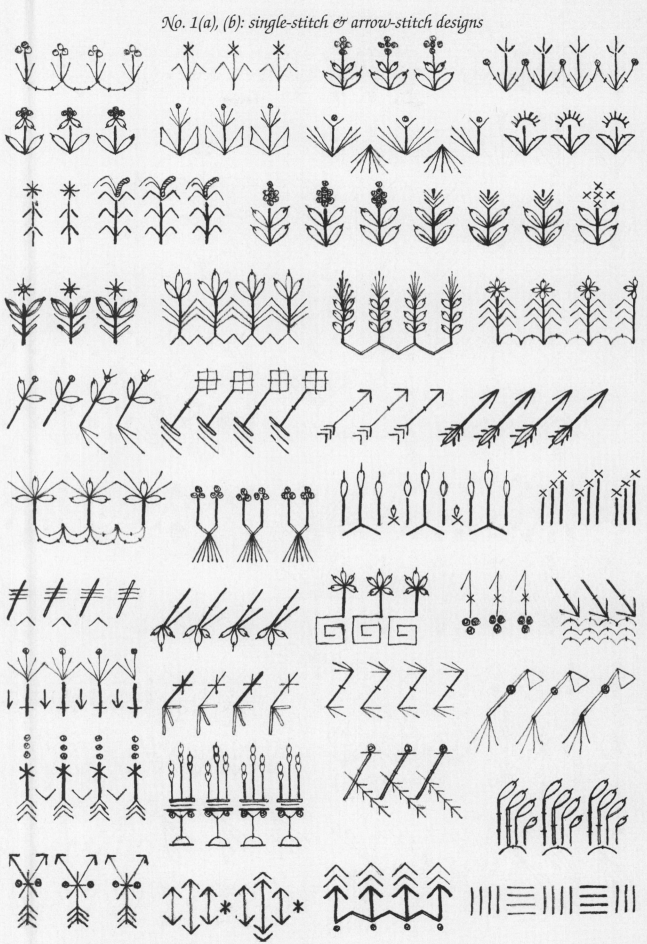

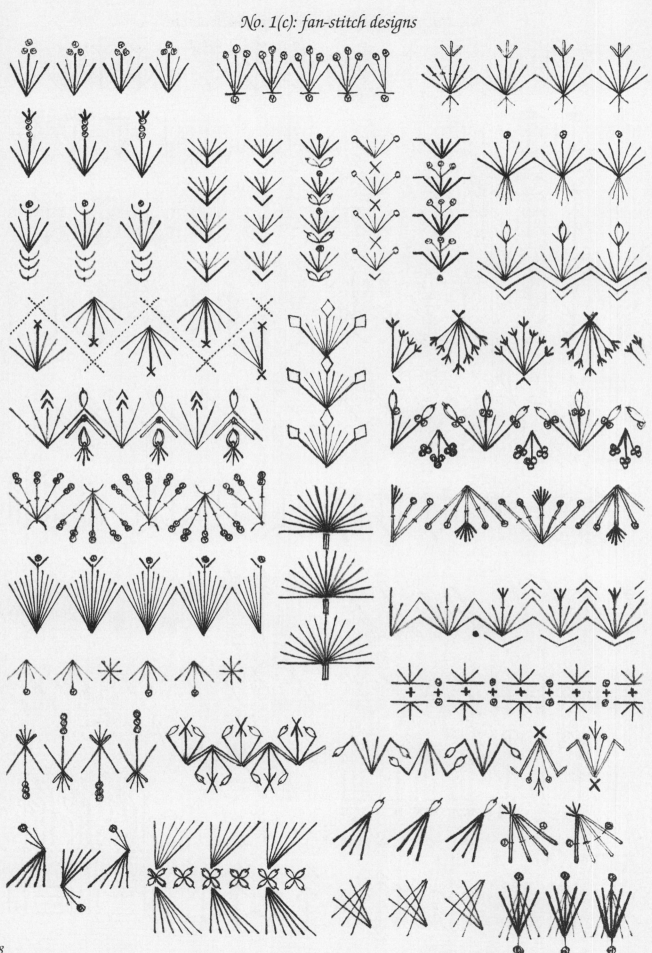

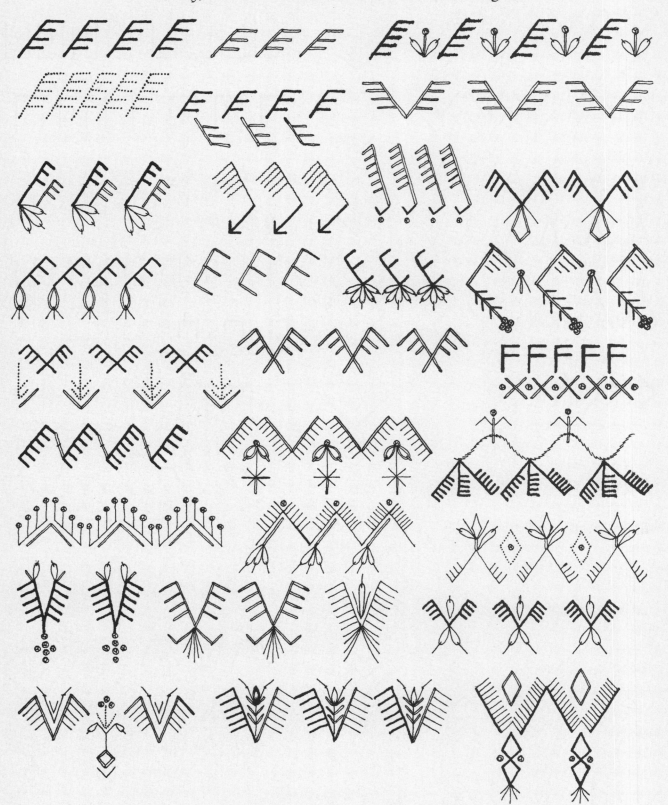

For comb designs: Work one long stitch, bringing the thread up at the seam to begin; then the uppermost tooth in the comb; then the remaining teeth with short, straight stitches. These are best worked toward the long stitch. In the last design, the teeth are worked in a finer thread than that used for the long stitches, but the color remains the same.

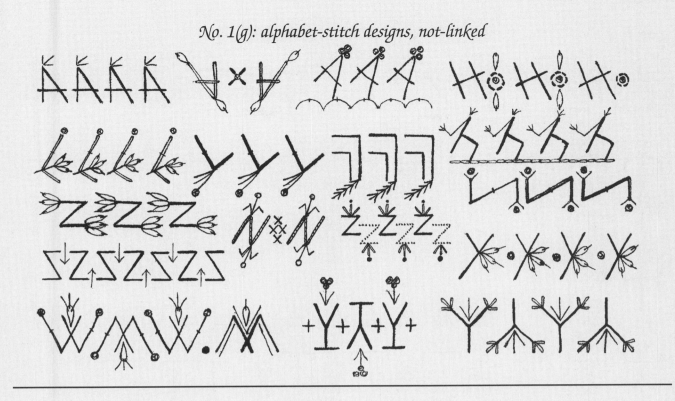

No. 1(h): linked alphabet-stitch designs

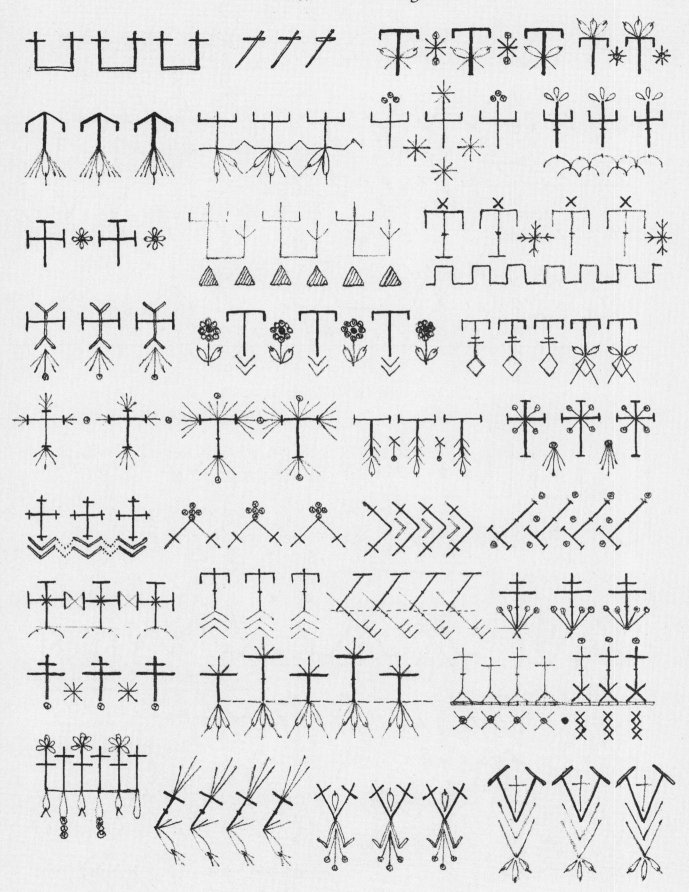

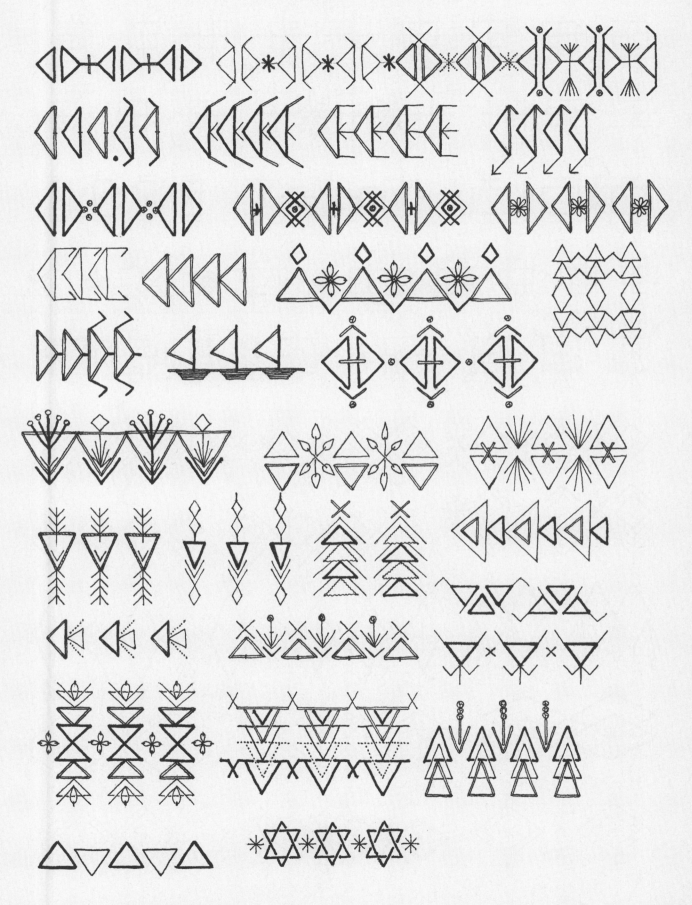

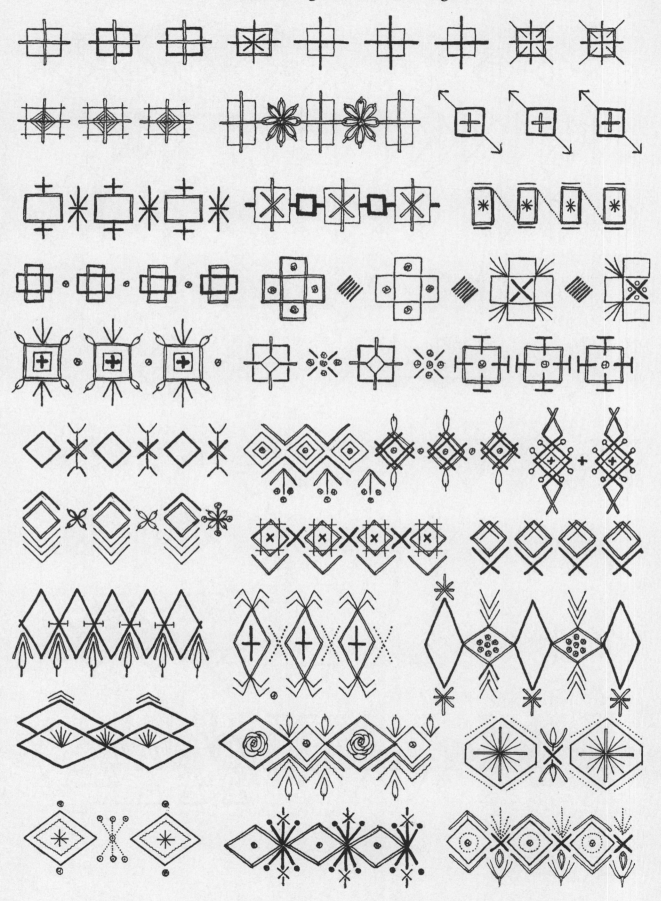

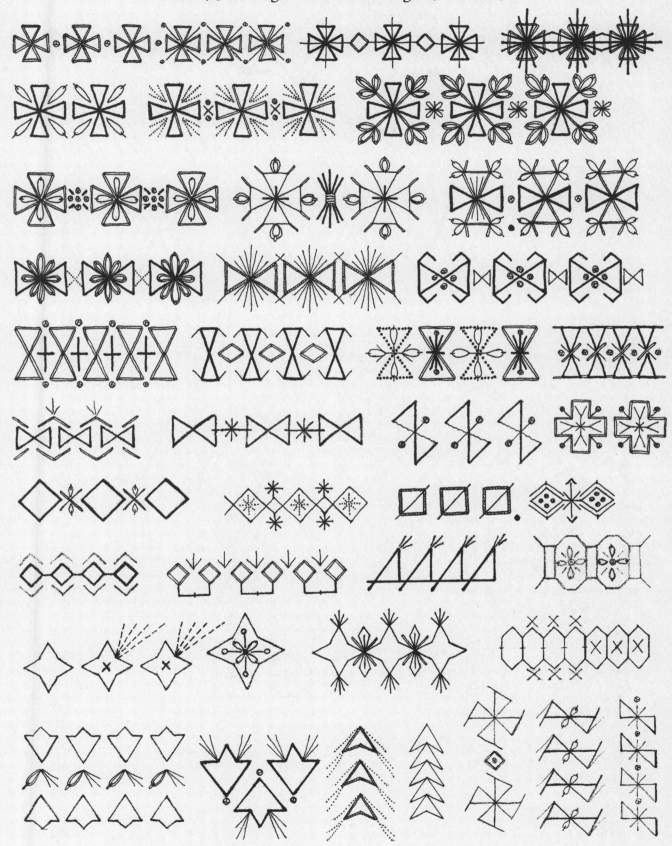

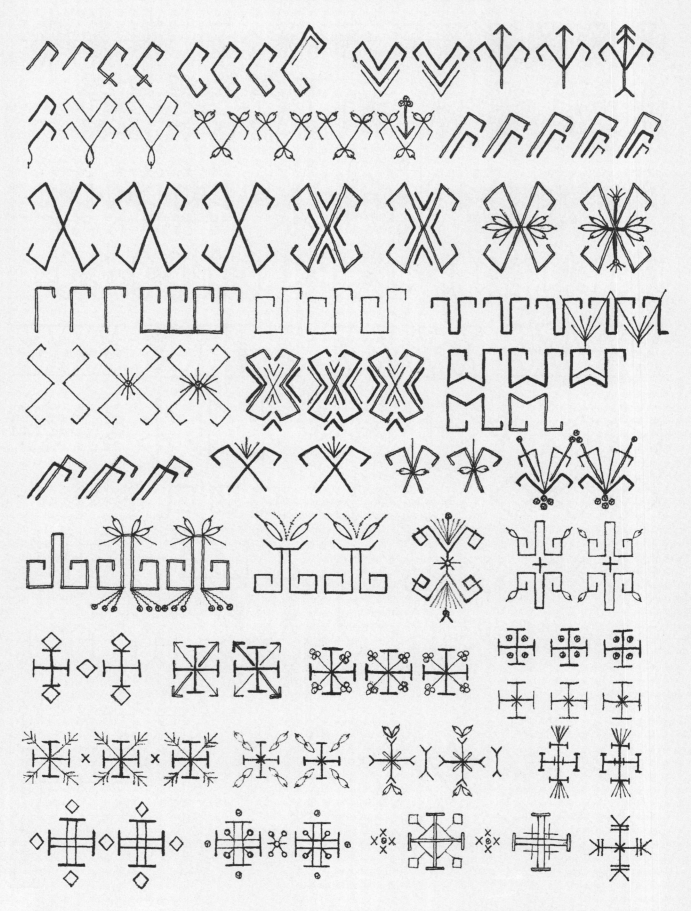

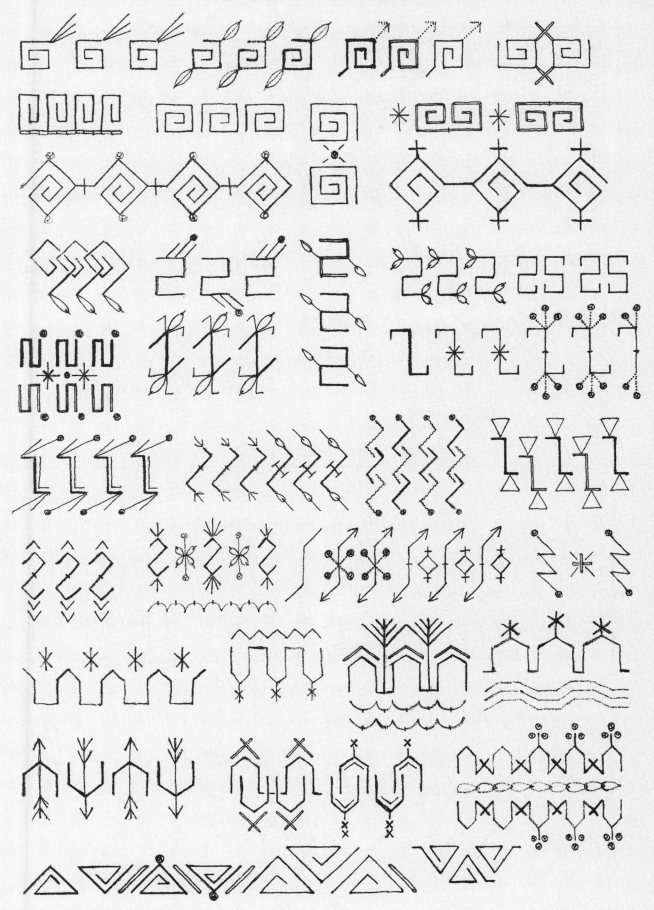

No. 1(m): criss-cross-stitch designs

No. 1(n): miscellaneous straight-stitch designs

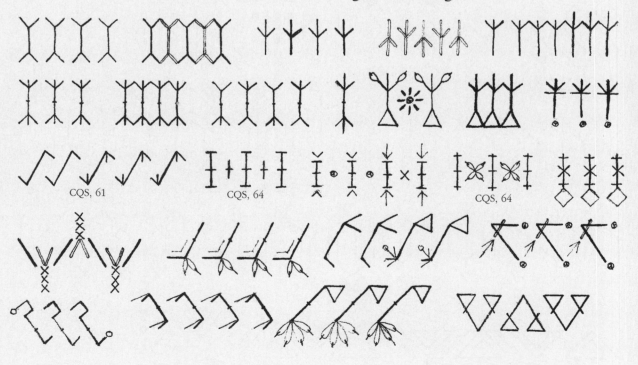

CQS, 61

CQS, 64

CQS, 64

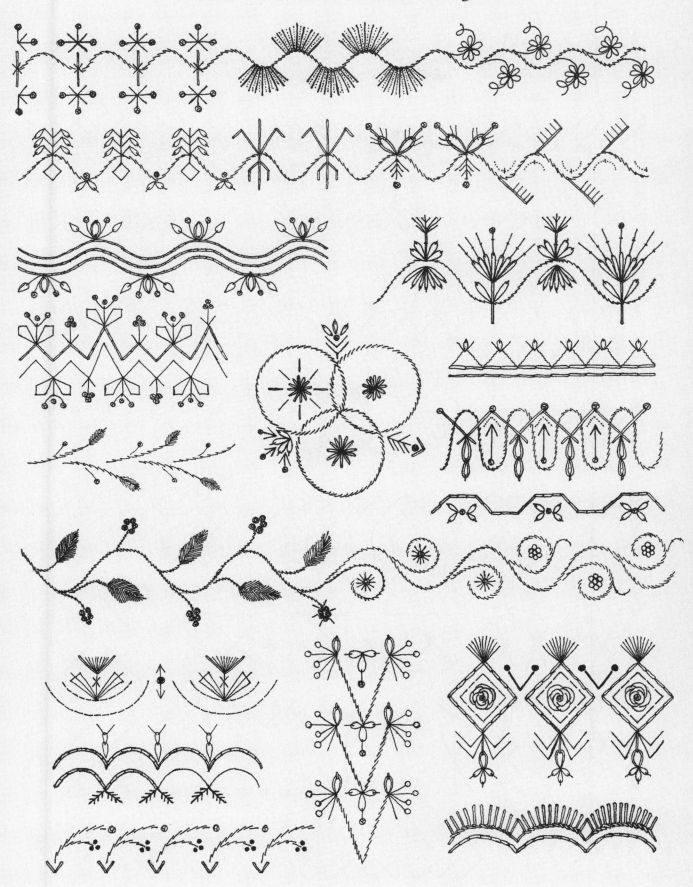

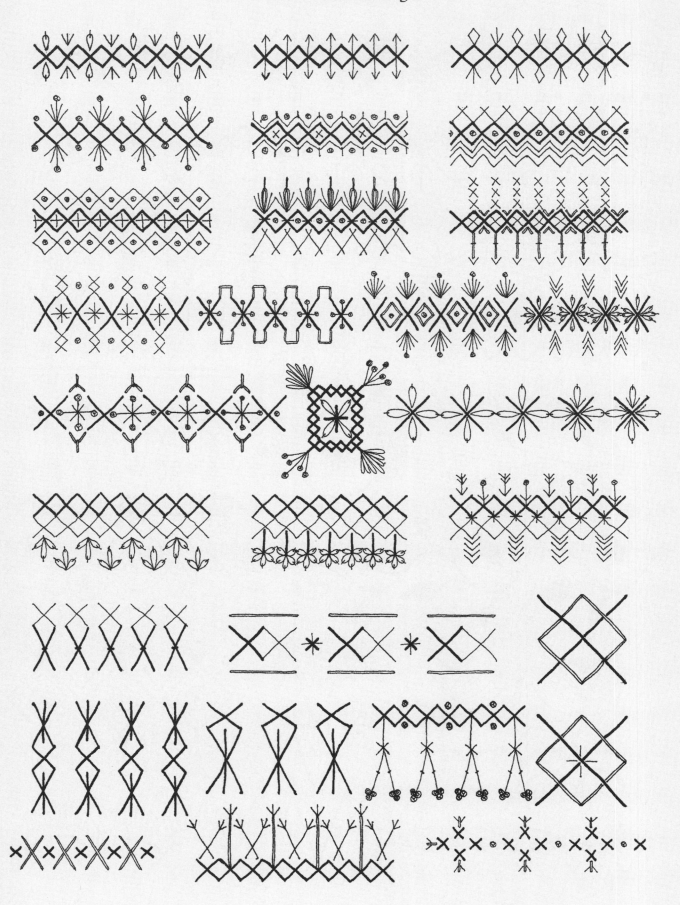

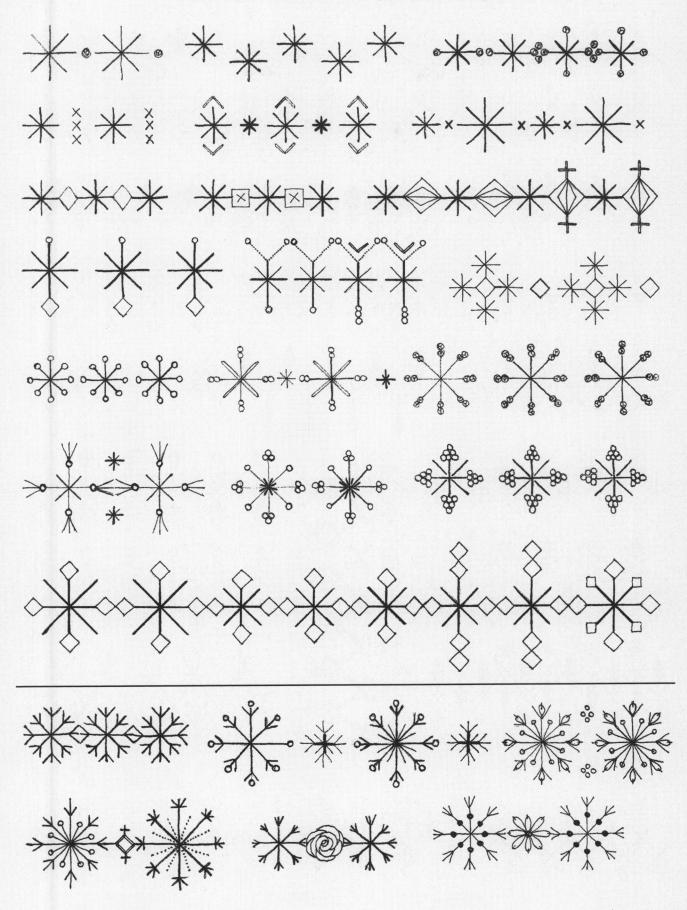

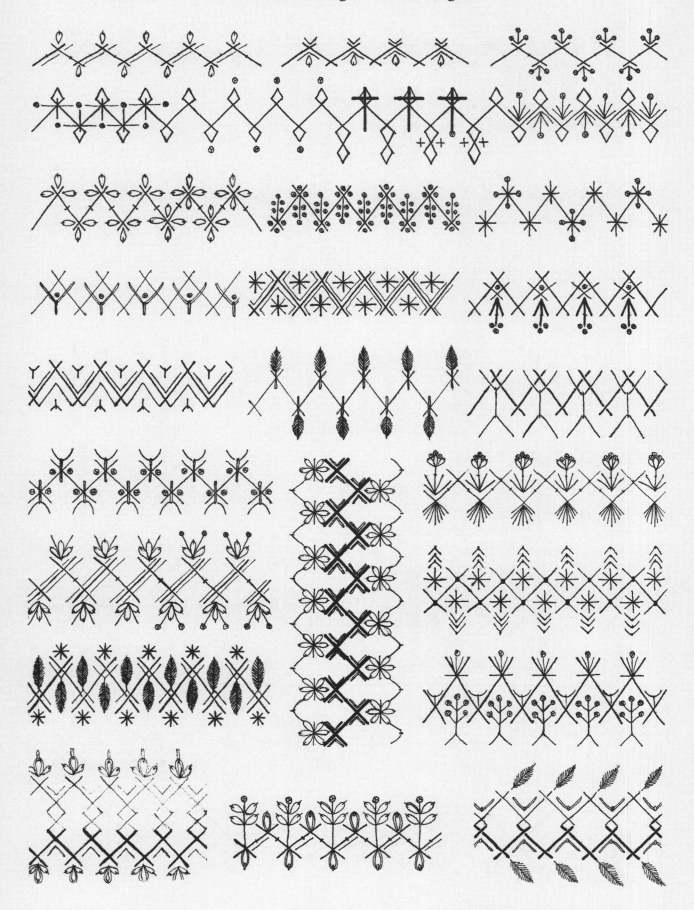

No. 7(b): detached herringbone-stitch designs

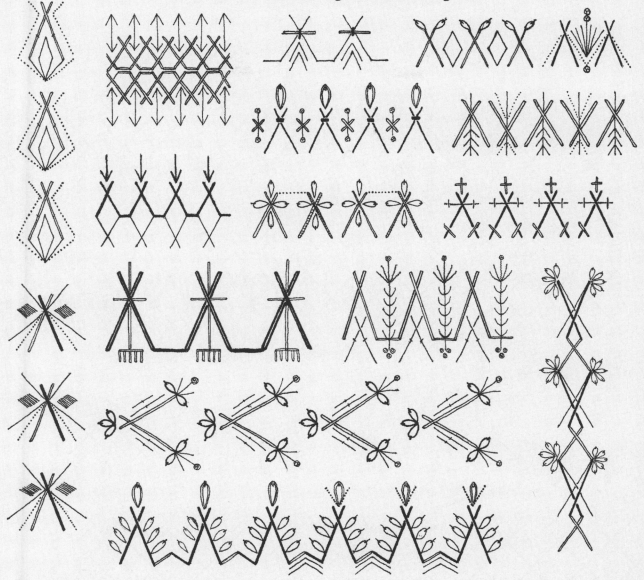

No. 8: backstitched herringbone-stitch designs

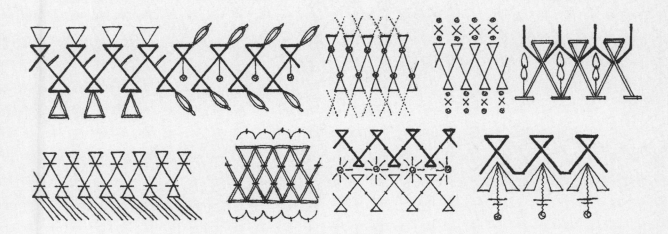

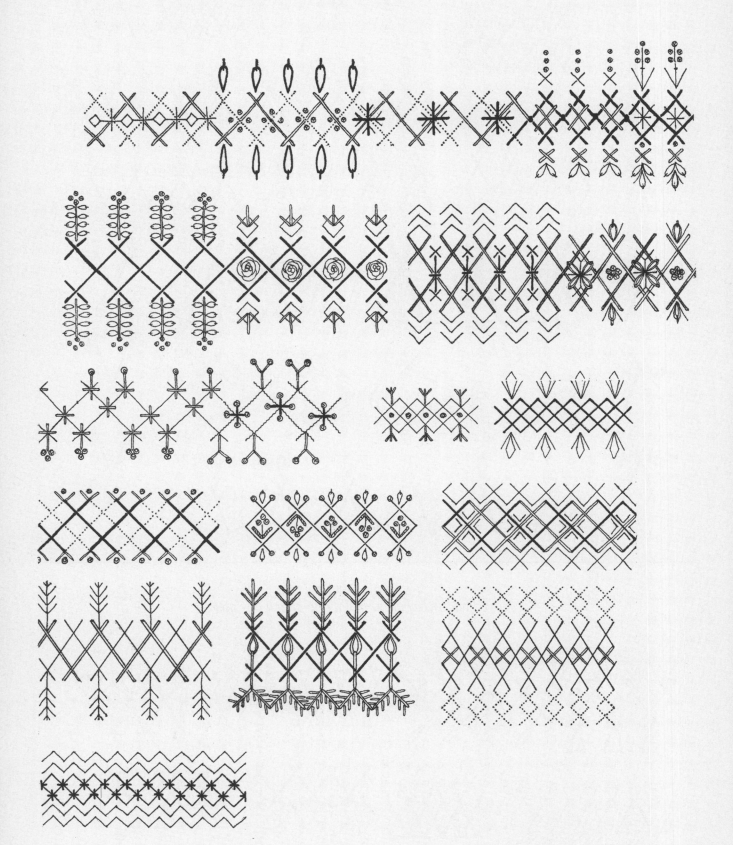

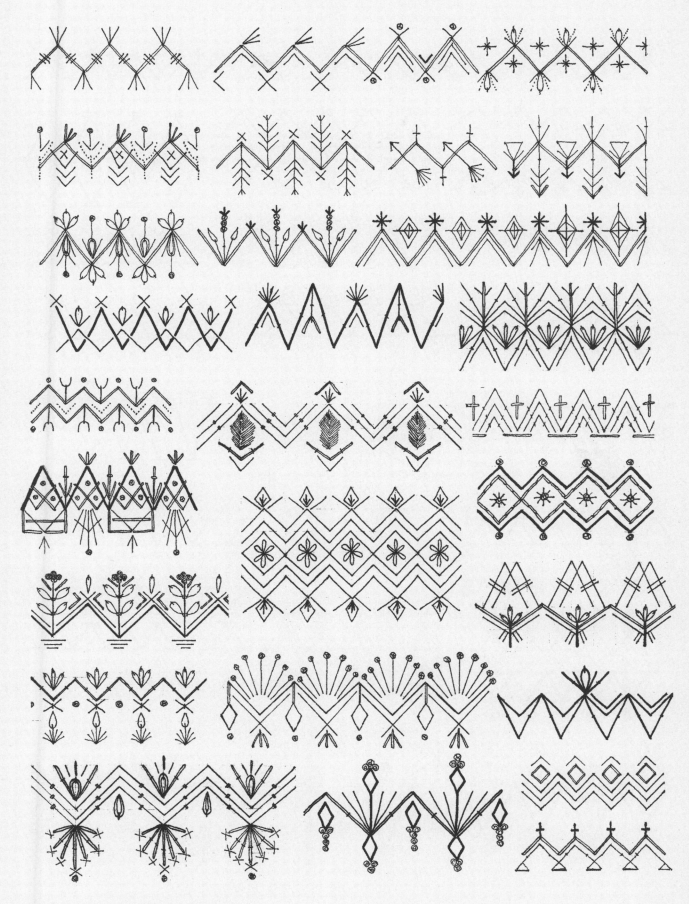

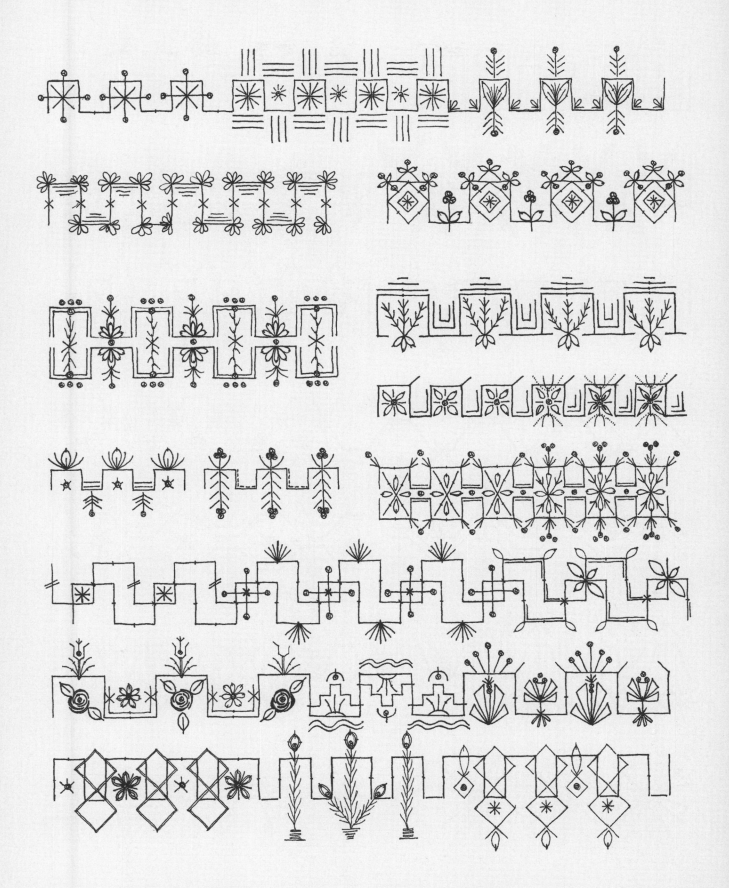

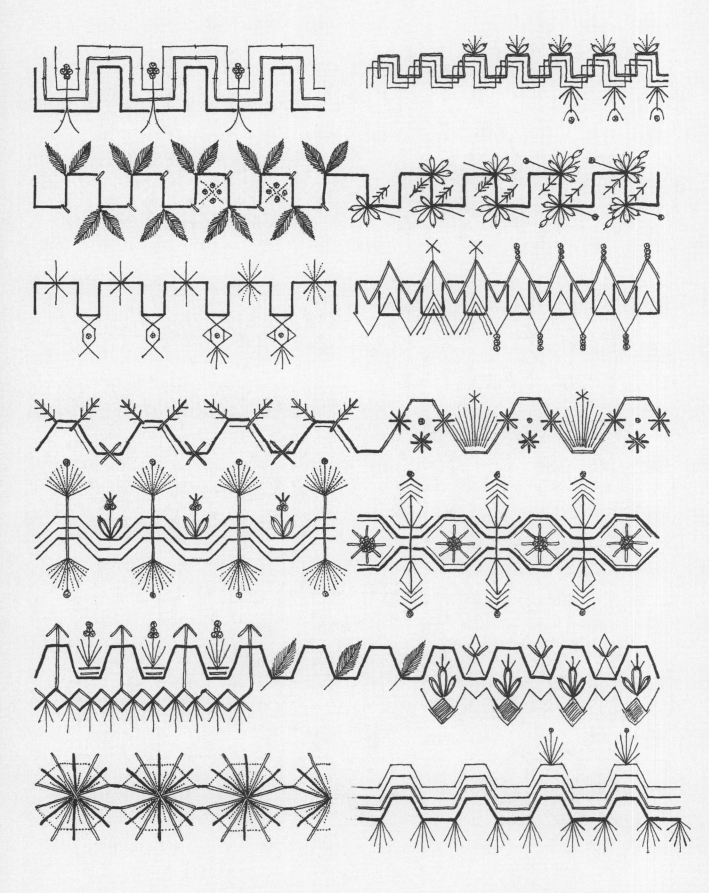

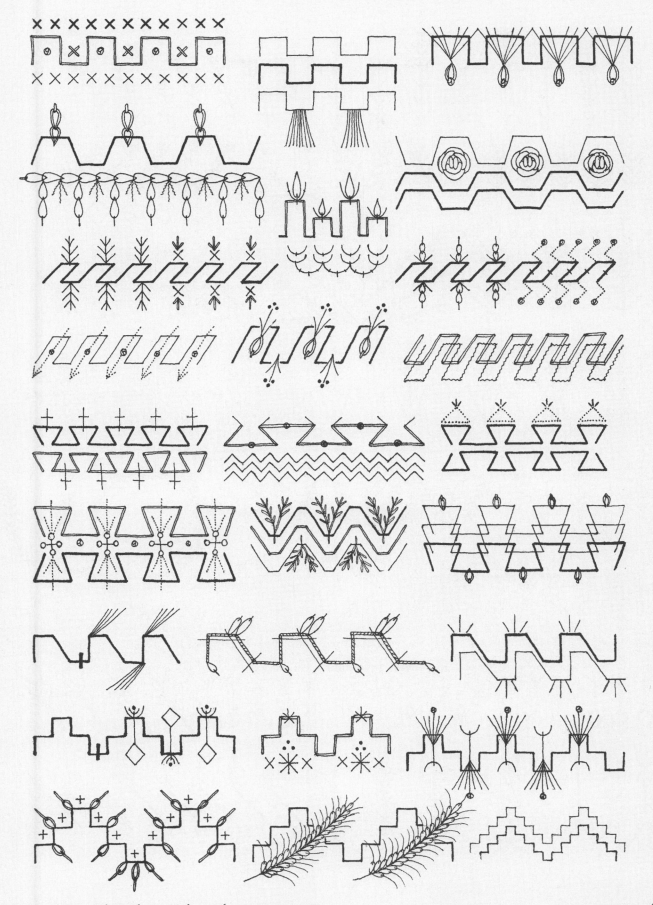

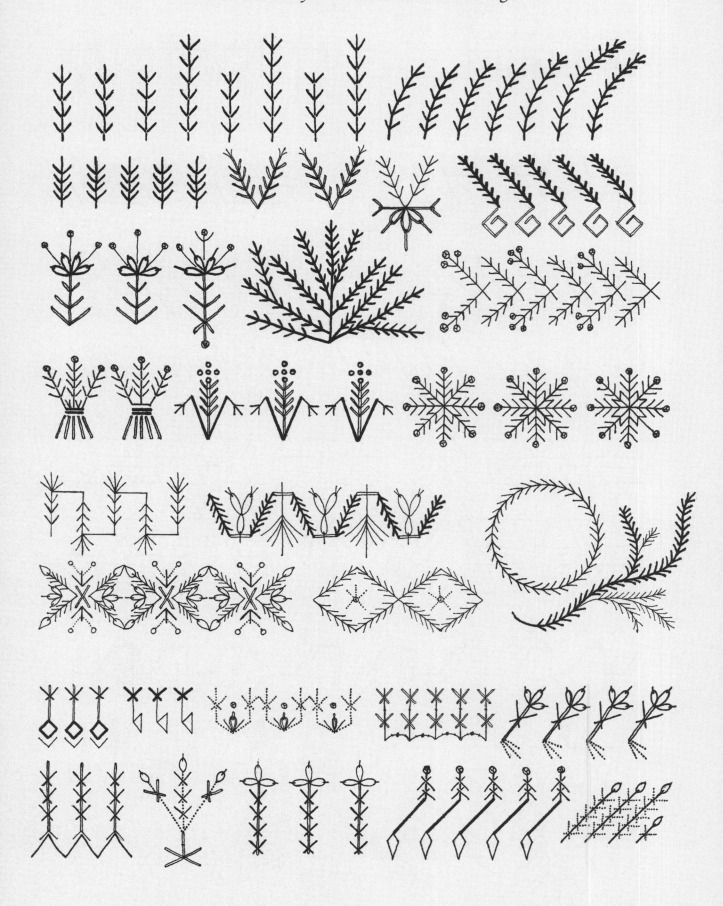

No. 16: zigzag-stitch designs

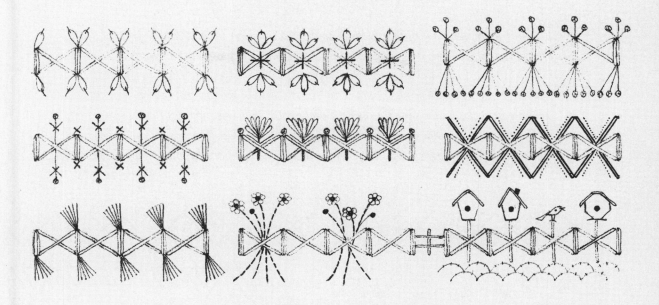

No. 17: fishbone leaf-stitch designs

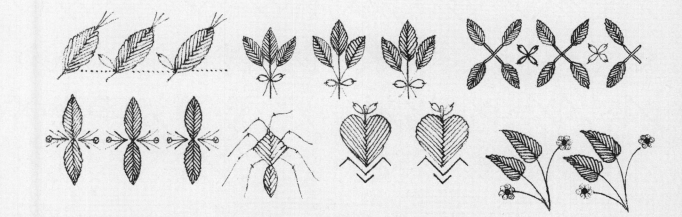

No. 18: satin-stitch designs

CQS, 81

As I worked on my third and most ambitious sampler, I realized near the end of the project that something was missing. It needed a border or embroidered frame of some kind to contain and unify the diverse design elements already stitched. These newly created stitcheries are different from the standard linear variety. As you can see, most of them are composed of an open or closed geometric shape with only one dominant embellisher and, perhaps, one subordinate embellisher. They have a somewhat more masculine appeal and are gorgeous when worked in an over-dyed thread, as I did on the much-improved sampler.

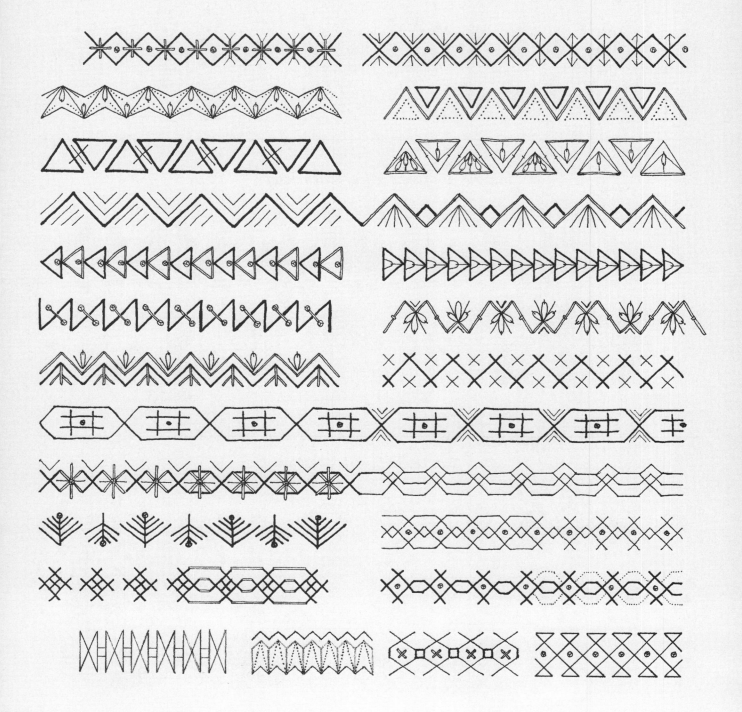

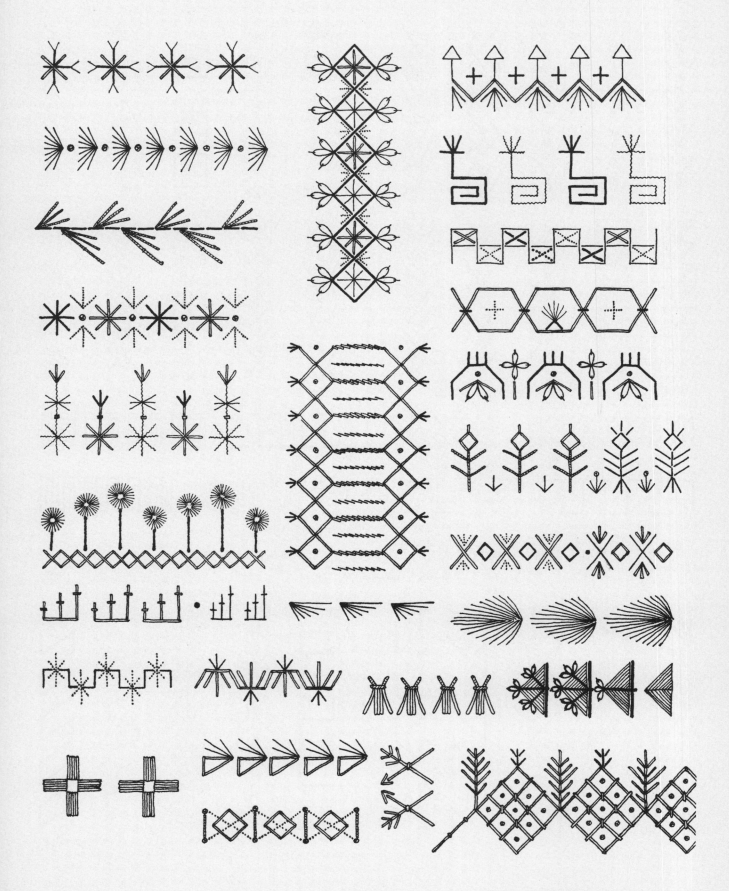

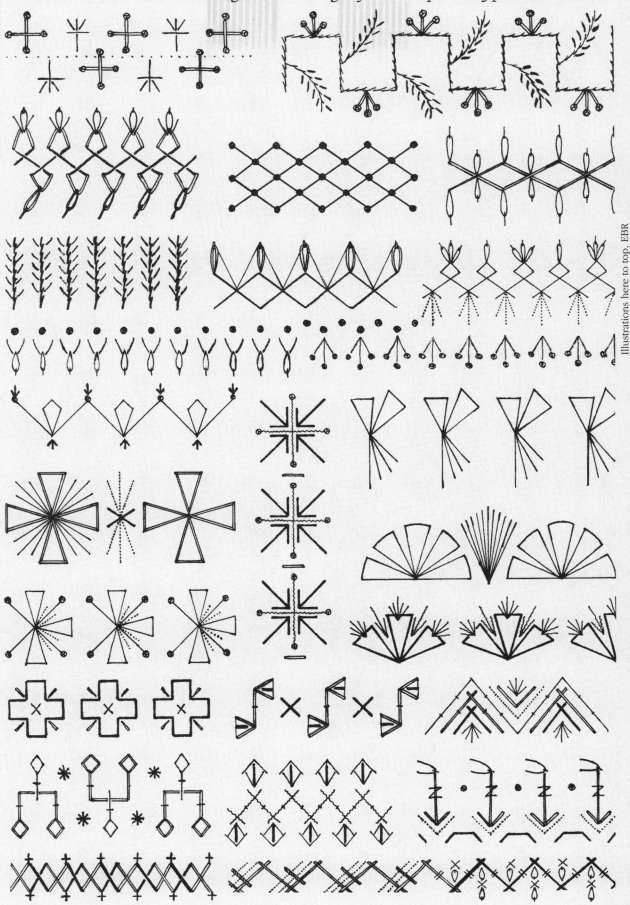

Illustrations here to top, EBR

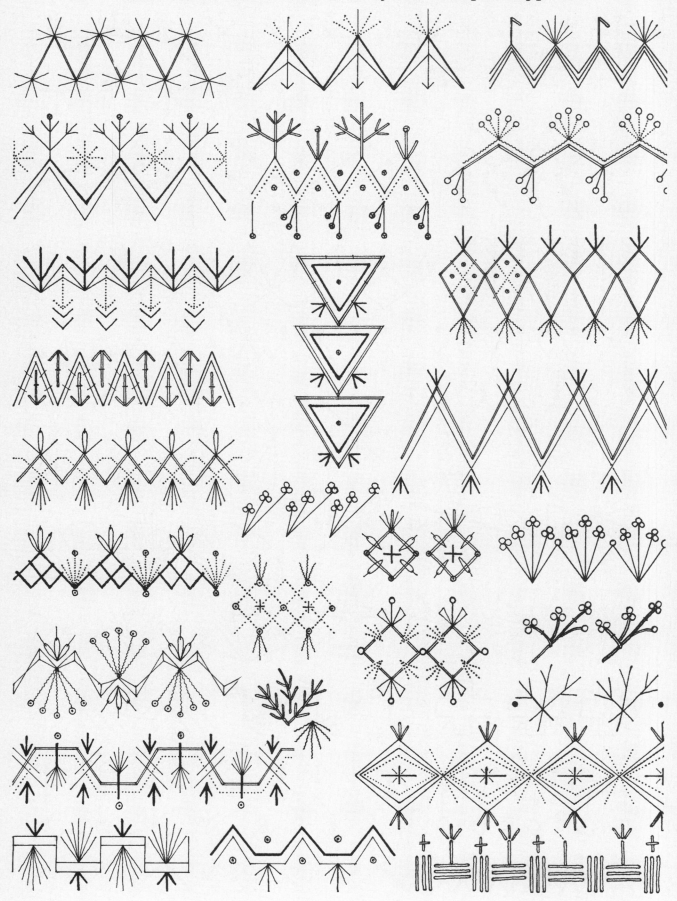

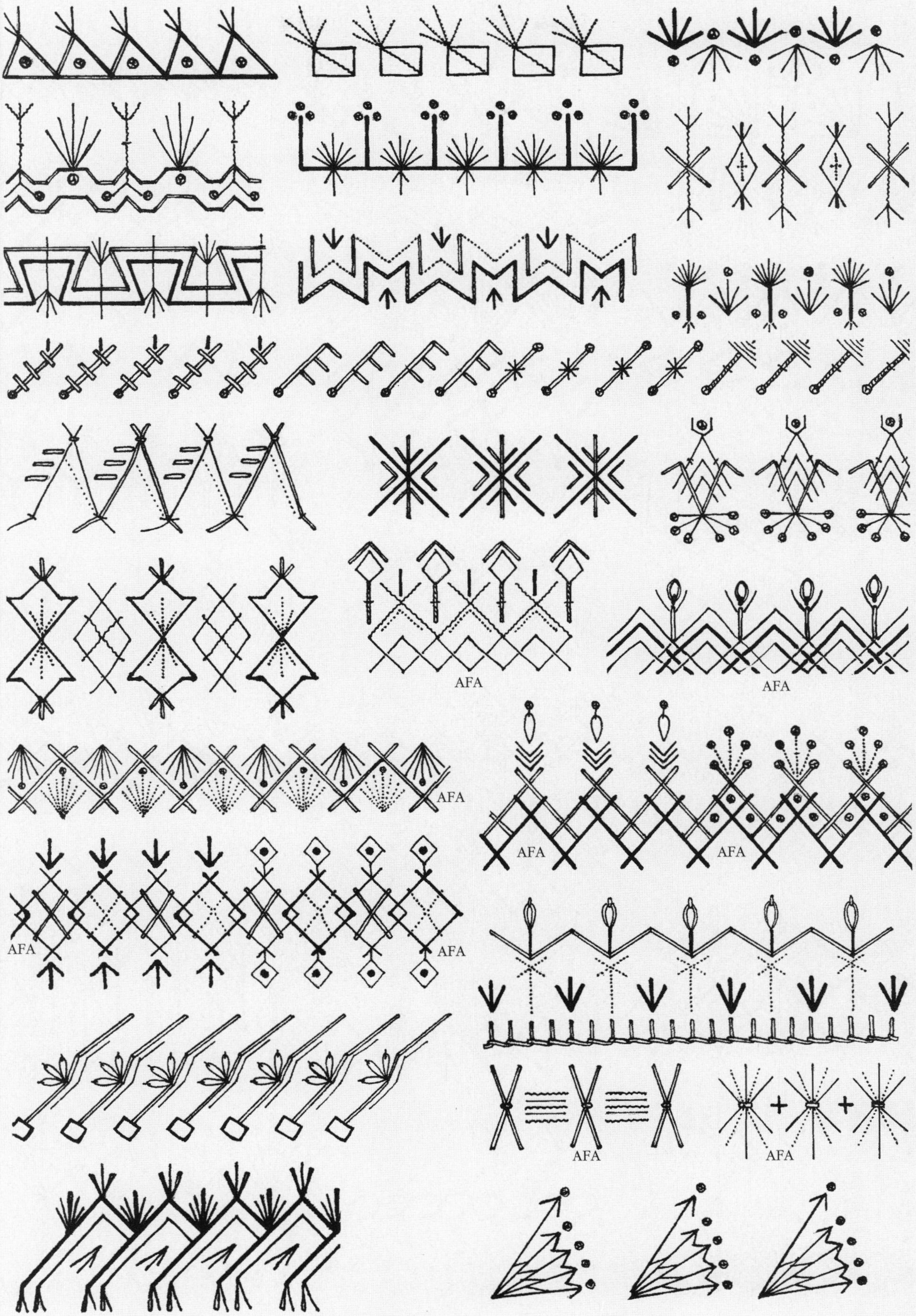

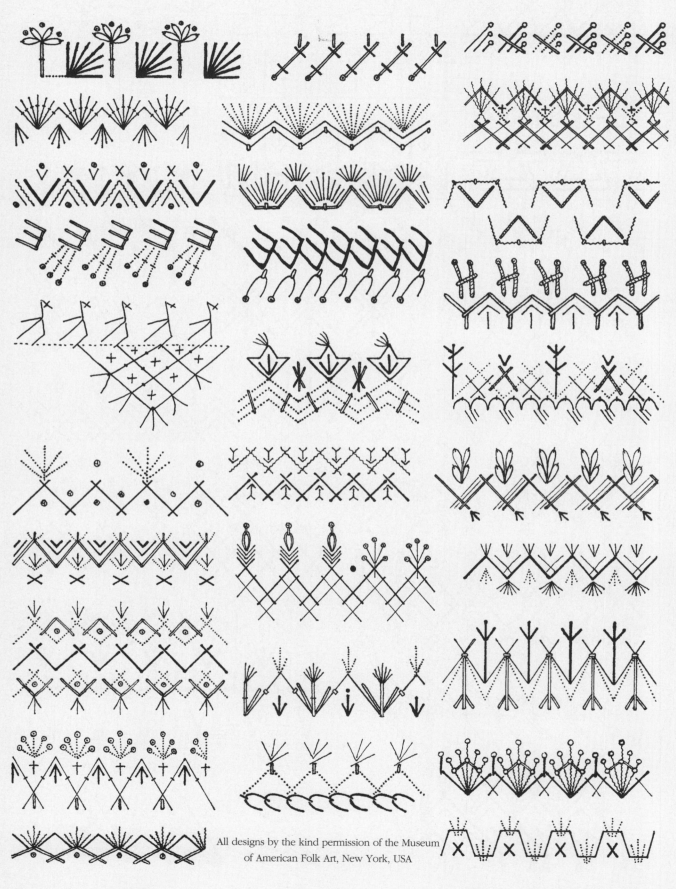

All designs by the kind permission of the Museum
of American Folk Art, New York, USA

Treasury of Crazyquilt Stitches...Carole Samples

1/8" (3mm) ribbon

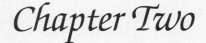

Chapter Two

Blanket-Stitch &
Feather-Stitch Designs

Detail of crazywork panel, by the author, 1997

Demystifying the feather stitches,
or, a blanket stitch by any other name...

There are pages and pages of notes in my teacher's notebook regarding the 15 members of Basic Stitch Group Two, but most of that data can be compressed into a handful of very important observations. The stitches numbered 21 through 35 in the Treasury are, as already stated, second only to Group One stitches in frequency of use.

We will begin our study with the simple, generic blanket stitch (Illus. 2-1). The Dictionary catalogs 30 distinct forms of stitch No. 21 as it is worked along many SBLs with varying orientations for its individual upright stitches. (Stitches No. 22 and No. 23 are special configurations of the blanket stitch, of course.) Yet, as impressive as are these many possible primary stitches, the most remarkable of all the stitches in this group is, without question, the seldom-discussed alternating blanket stitch, for upon its third standard form all of the feather stitches are based.

Every true feather stitch is really an alternating blanket stitch on a zigzagging stitchery base line. Once you realize this extraordinary fact and begin to test it visually during your close encounters with crazyquilts, you will soon come to see how similar the several feather stitches are and how they differ, and how they may all be worked with certain success.

Illustrations 2-2 and 2-3 present the first and second generic formats of alternating blanket stitch. Their difference is obvious. In Illus. 2-4, we come to the heart of my bold observation, quite literally. No matter how many "alternating upright" stitches are worked on either side of the SBL, so long as they are worked in the same size orientation and in a natural (that is to say, not overly large) size, a true feather stitch will result. As many as six "uprights" may be clustered on opposite sides of the SBL segments; however, two or three "uprights" repeating is the most common configuration on antique quilts.

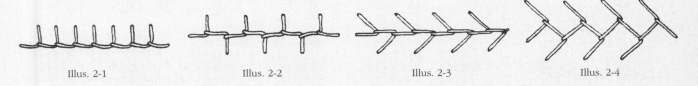

Illus. 2-1   Illus. 2-2   Illus. 2-3   Illus. 2-4

Traditionally, the interval between individual upright stitches in all members of Basic Stitch Group Two remains consistently the same length throughout the entire stitchery. The angle between a "zig" and its adjacent "zag" in feather stitches (also known as the SBL segment angle) is always the same as well; at least, we try to make it so.

Virtually all of the designs in Chapter Two are drawn as if worked by a right-handed stitcher. Thus, every blanket and alternating blanket stitch variation begins at the far left directly on each stitchery base line by bringing the needle and thread up and all the way out of the cloth at that point, regardless of whether the entire stitchery lies along the seam or whether it takes shape as a circle or continuous spiral or multiple-diagonal-rows formation (also along a seam). Left-handers reverse this direction and stitch from right to left along the chosen pathway. Remember to couch wherever needed in order to maintain a curved SBL if there are no actual upright stitches to accomplish this purpose.

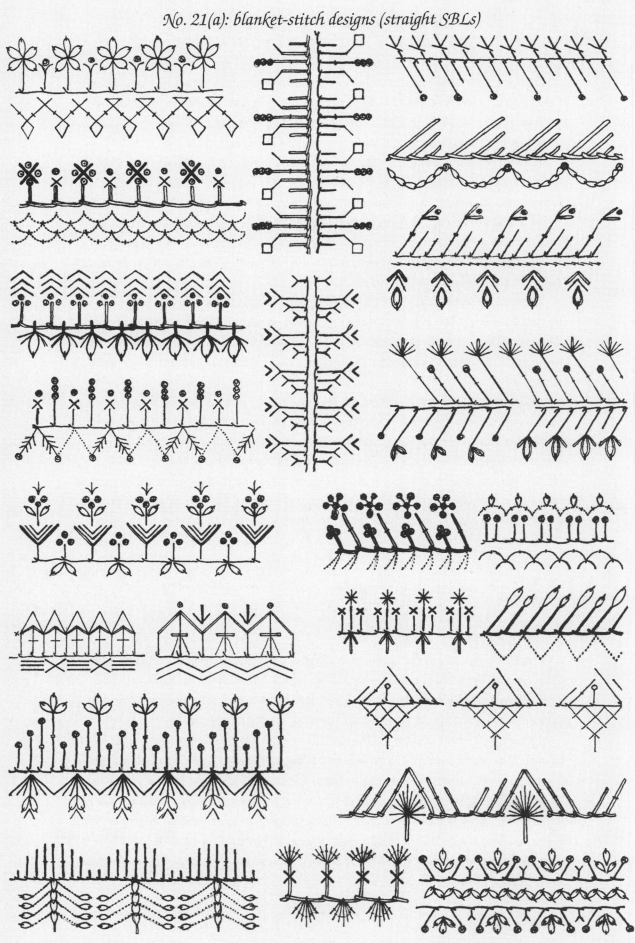

Treasury of Crazyquilt Stitches...Carole Samples

No. 21(a), (b): blanket-stitch designs (straight SBLs & diagonal-on-the-seam)

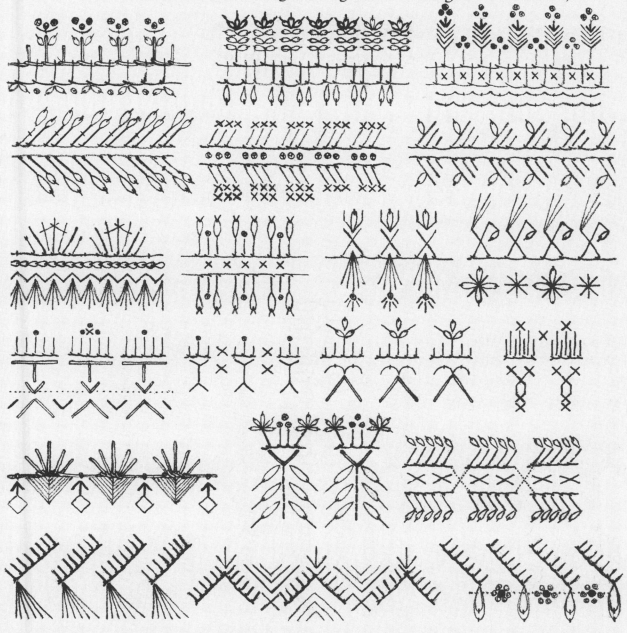

No. 22: buttonhole stitch designs (straight, serpentine, & scalloped SBLs)

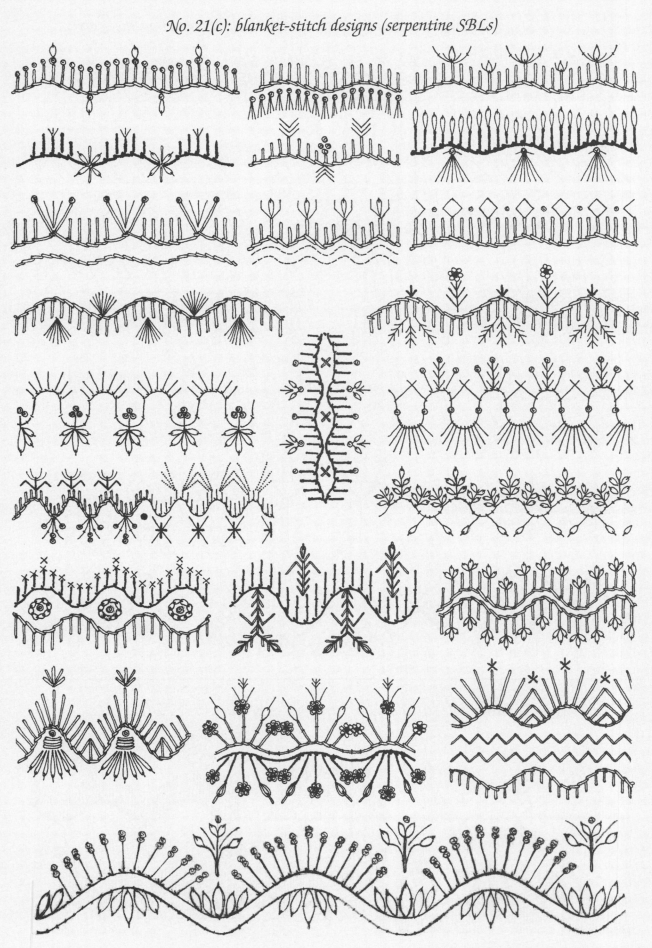

Treasury of Crazyquilt Stitches...Carole Samples

No. 21(d), (e): blanket-stitch designs (Holbein and zigzagging SBLs)

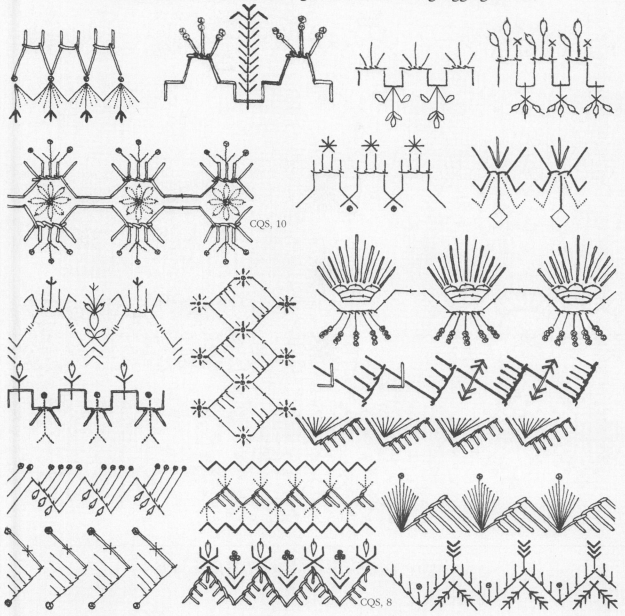

CQS, 10

CQS, 8

No. 23: broad-band zigzagging blanket-stitch designs

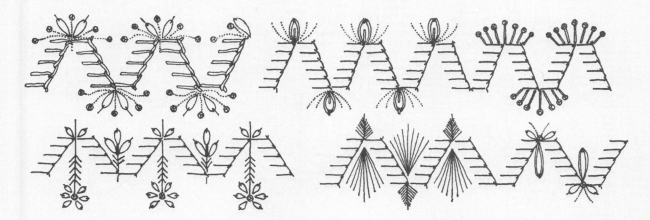

No. 21(f), (g): blanket-stitch designs (scalloping & circular SBLs)

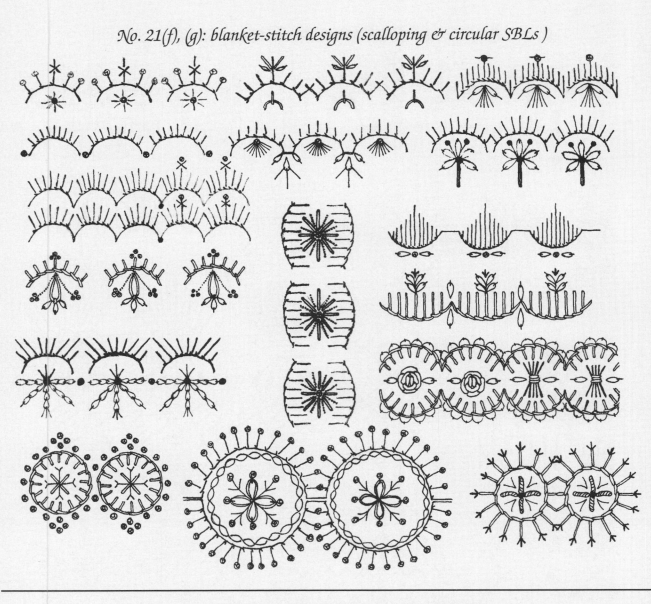

No. 21(h): blanket-stitch designs (free-form SBLs)

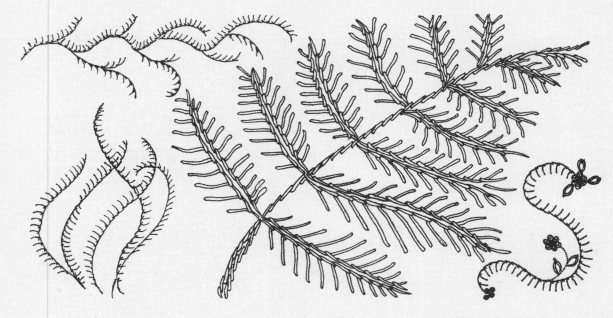

Treasury of Crazyquilt Stitches...Carole Samples

No. 24: closed blanket-stitch designs (straight SBLs)

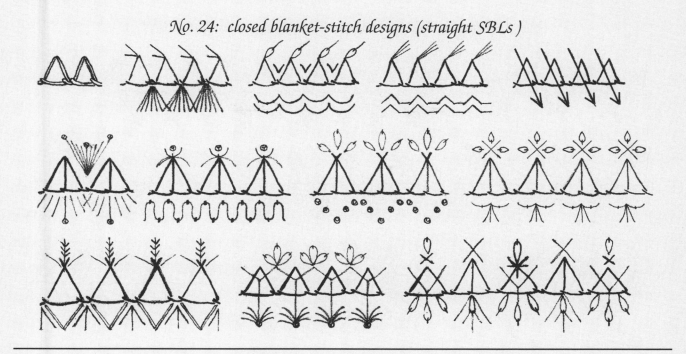

No. 25 (a), (b): closed blanket-stitch designs (curved SBLs & clamshell stitches)

CQS, 12

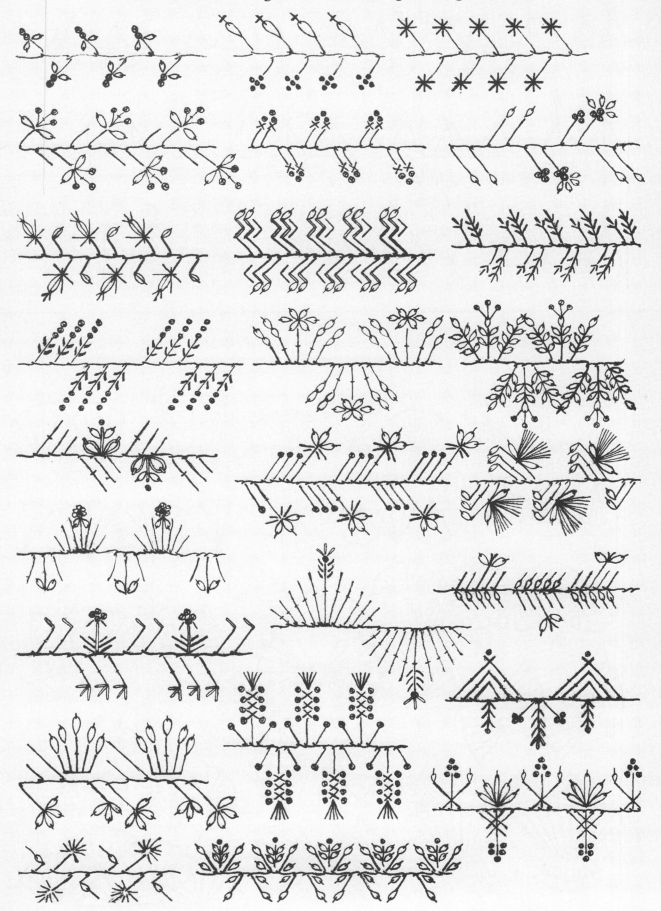

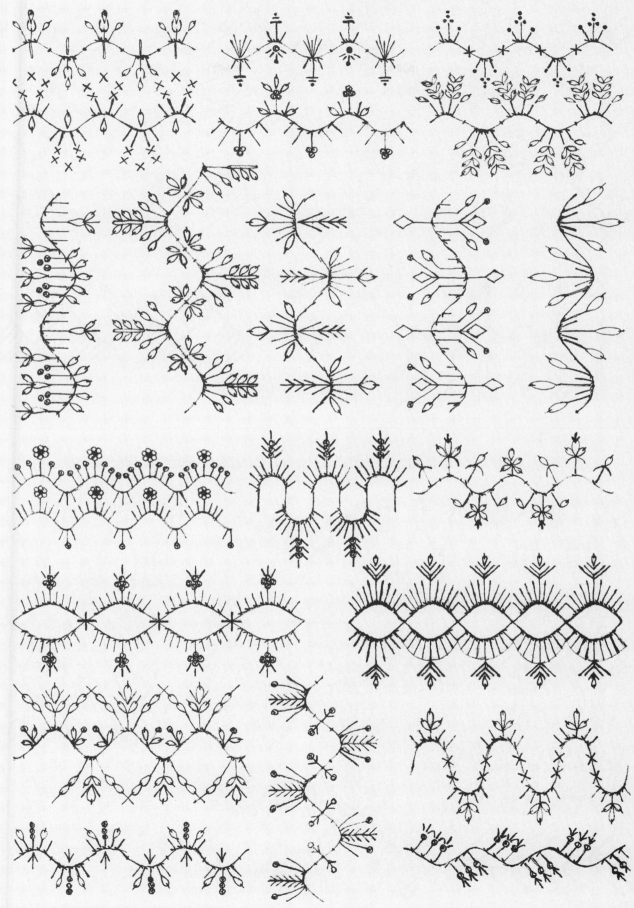

No. 26(c): alternating blanket-stitch designs (zigzagging SBLs)

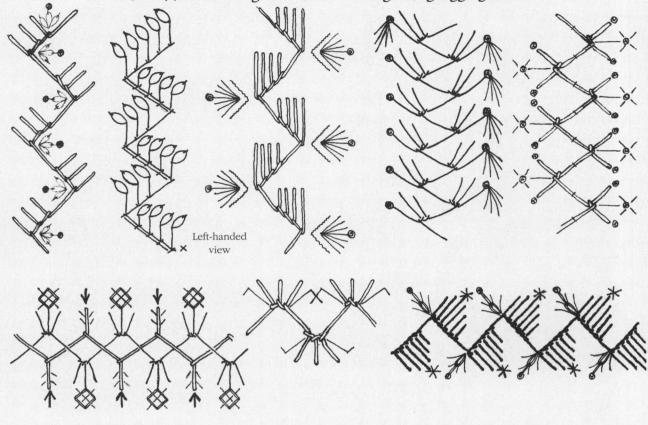

Left-handed view

No. 26(d), (e): alternating blanket-stitch designs (Holbein & other traditional SBLs)

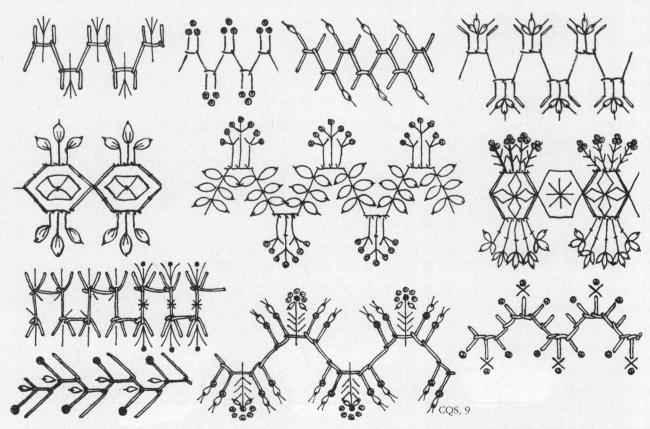

CQS, 9

Treasury of Crazyquilt Stitches…Carole Samples

No. 27: long-armed feather-stitch designs • No. 28: maidenhair-stitch designs

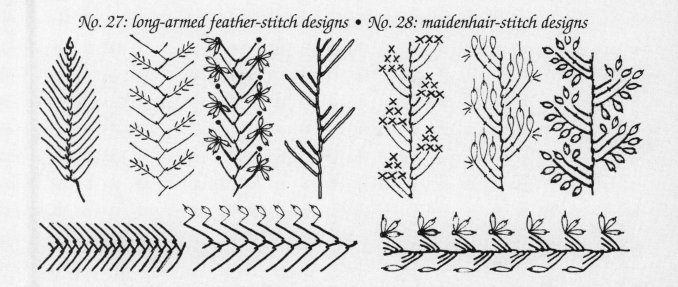

No. 29(a), (b), (c): straight feather-stitch designs (single, double & triple variations)

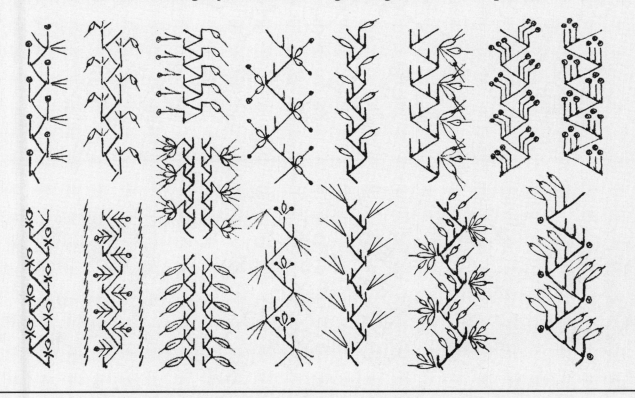

No. 30: common feather-stitch designs

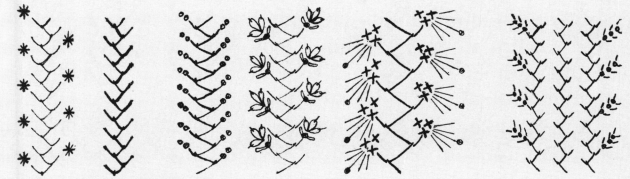

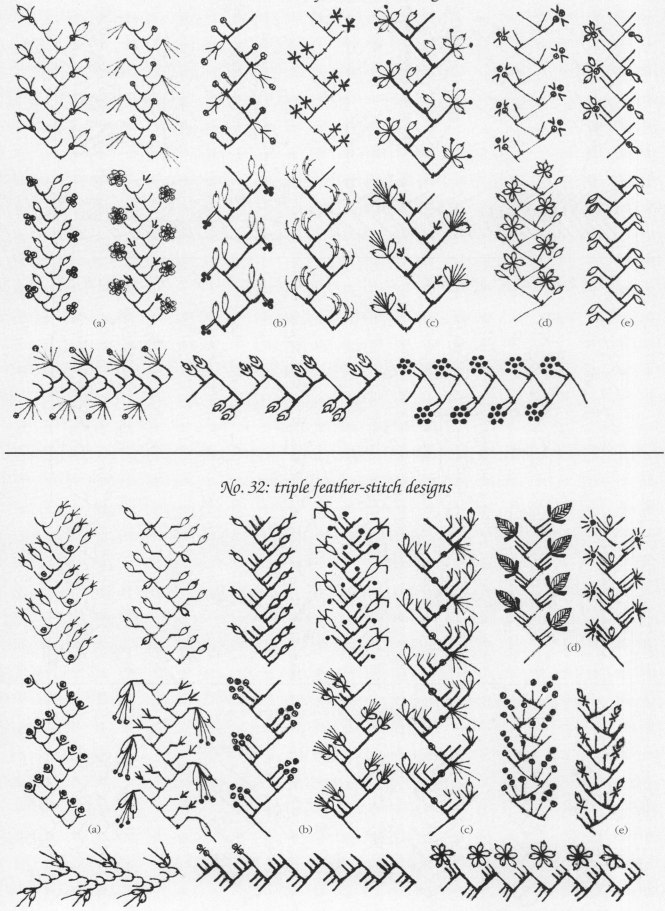

No. 31: double feather-stitch designs

(a) (b) (c) (d) (e)

No. 32: triple feather-stitch designs

(a) (b) (c) (d) (e)

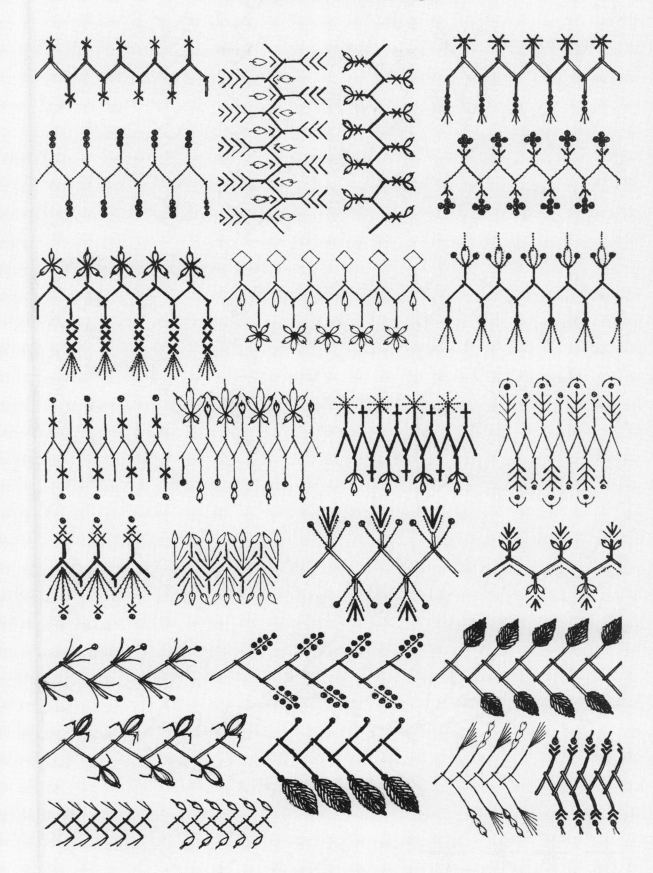

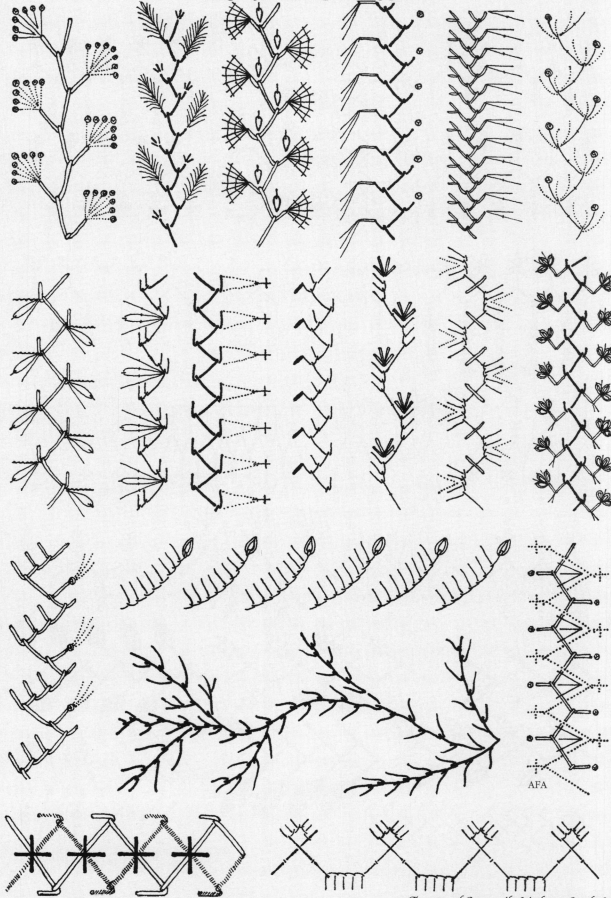

AFA

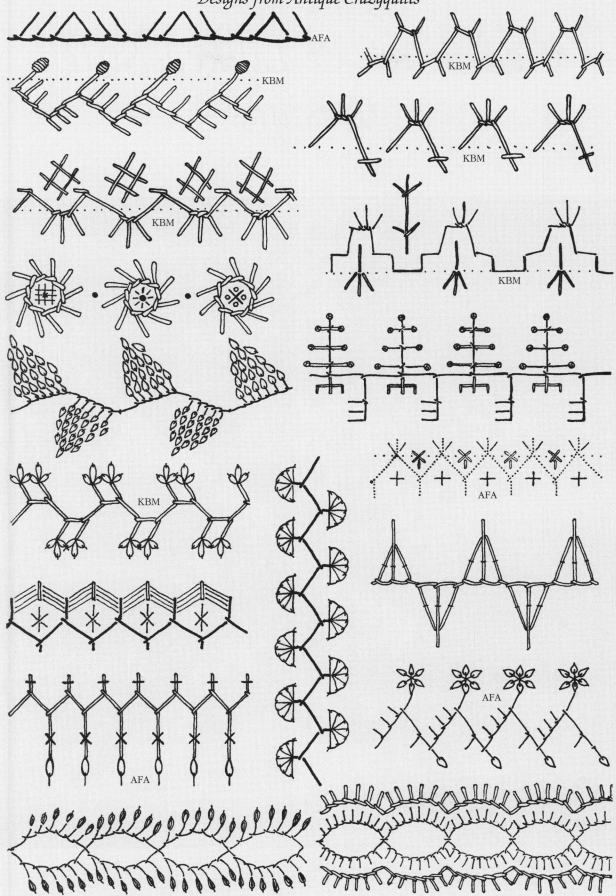

Chapter Three

Tied-Stitch & Linked-Stitch Designs

Crazyquilt block, by the author, 1992

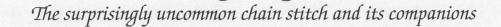

The surprisingly uncommon chain stitch and its companions

There are five primary stitches in Basic Stitch Group Three, and of these, four are beyond any doubt essential to contemporary crazyquilt embroidery. We begin with No. 36, the rather remarkable chain stitch. By definition and formation, this is an interconnected stitch, with each loop of thread caught and held in place by the very next loop in the chain except for the final loop, which is held by a tie stitch.

The resulting chain can be made to do all kinds of interesting things, and we rely on the various possible structures to decorate seams and patches alike. I have designed three pages of linear stitcheries which not only follow most of the standard base lines, but which also showcase the chain stitch in such traditional motifs as circles, squares, ellipses, diamonds, and hearts. In fact, an embroidered chain may conform to virtually any line one can draw, even a tight spiral to fill a particular shape. Yet, for all that, the chain stitch is second in importance to its close relative, the detached chain stitch.

This, our 37th stitch, is almost universally known as the lazy-daisy stitch and is arguably the most popular of all the embellisher stitches. Each detached chain consists of one loop, not linked to any other loop of thread, and held in place ordinarily by one tie stitch in any practical length (although sometimes, just for fun, I use two or three tie stitches on one loop). Notice that a loop may be either oval or round in shape, plump or skinny, long or short; and like an extra-long tie stitch, a loop might be couched on one or both sides to hold it in a certain position, as well as to help it retain one of the desired shapes.

Third on our list of essential Group Three stitches is No. 39 (a), the fly stitch. It was not used very often on nineteenth-century crazyquilts, but its rarity then cannot diminish its usefulness now for the embellishment of the seams and patches on crazywork items. Without its wide-bodied variation, which I have named the scalloping stitch, No. 39 (b), it would be very difficult to create delicate, realistic spiders' webs. It is invaluable as an outlining stitch for simple and complex spot motifs, but it also serves quite well in its occasional capacity as a primary stitch for contemporary seamwork.

Our two remaining primaries, feathered chain stitch (No. 38) and closed fly stitch (No. 40), are outstanding choices for crazyquilts, albeit they are not traditional to the genre. The first of these is composed of individual detached chain stitches with long tie stitches that are set together in a simple zigzagging configuration just like feather stitches, while the latter is really a group of closely stacked fly stitches, which together create excellent leaves. Both stitches are also easy to learn.

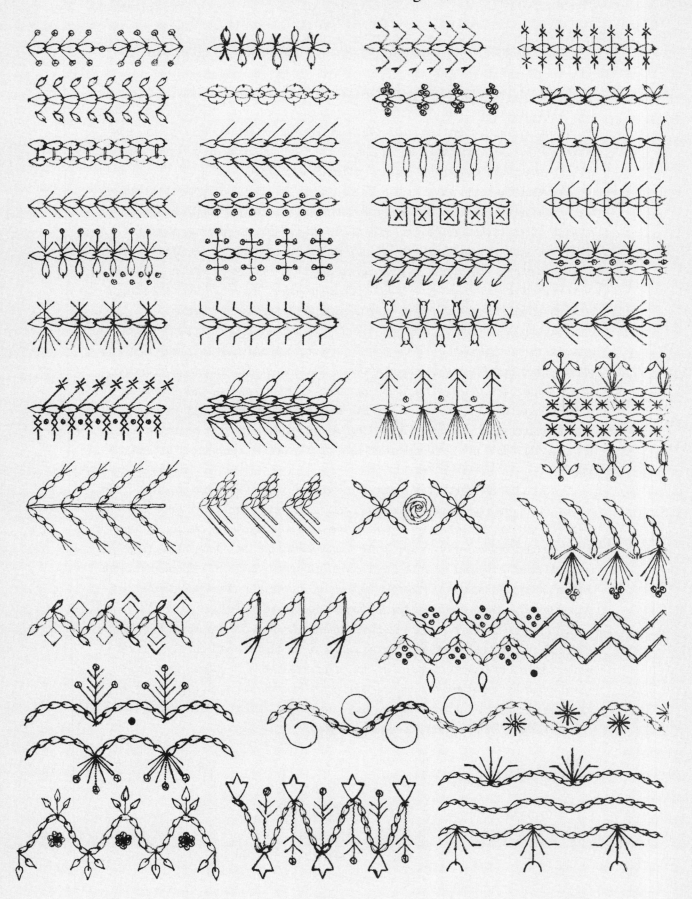

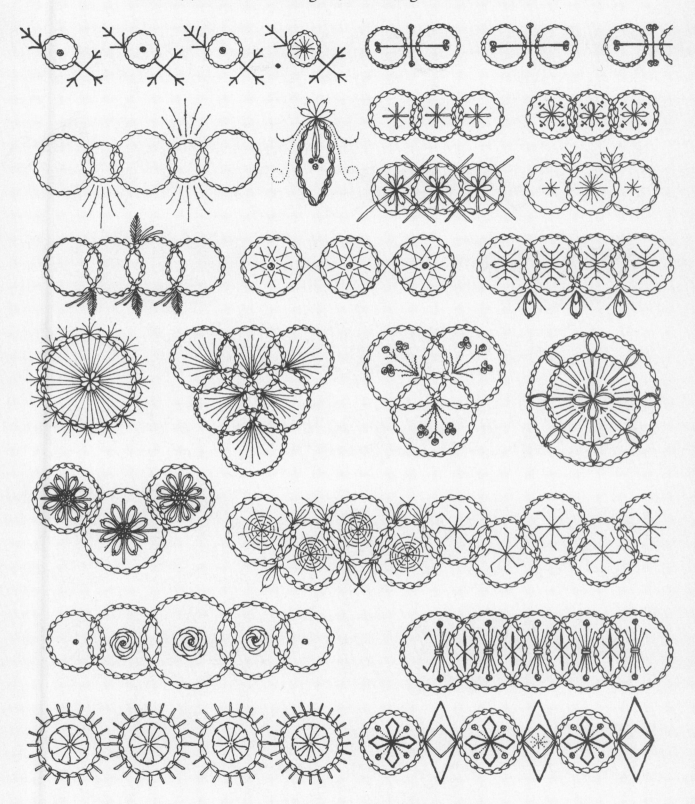

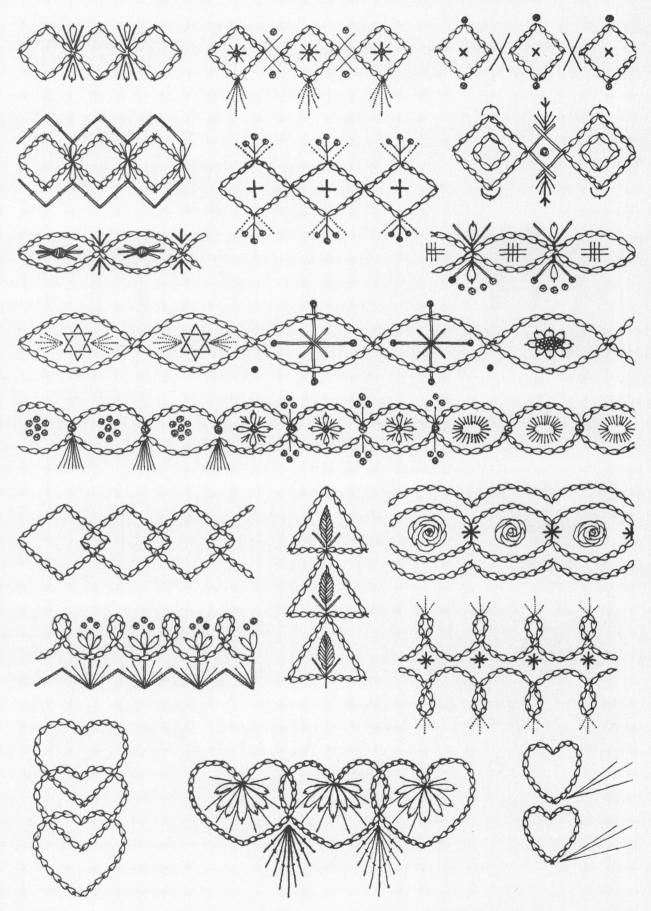

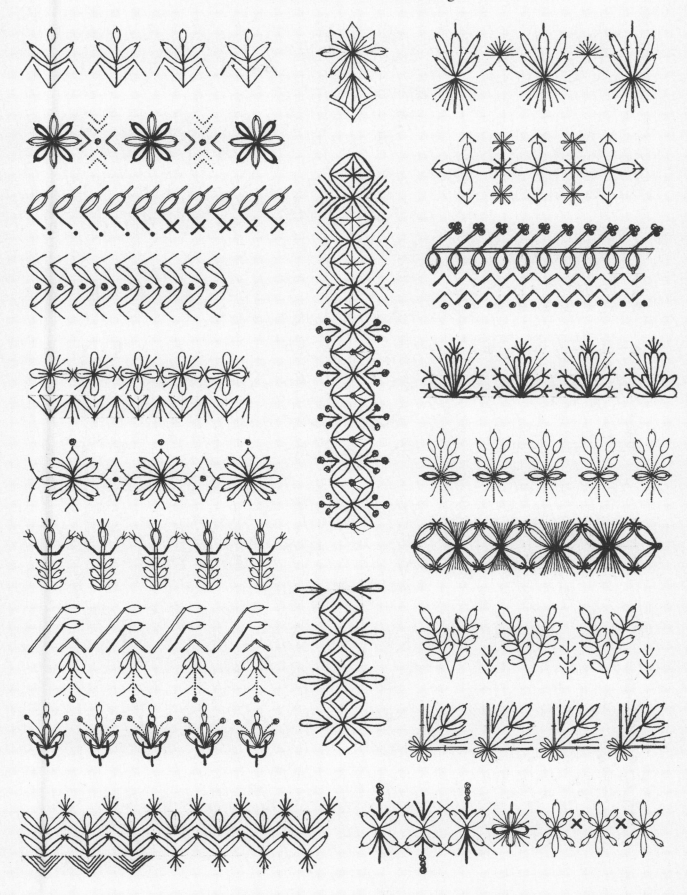

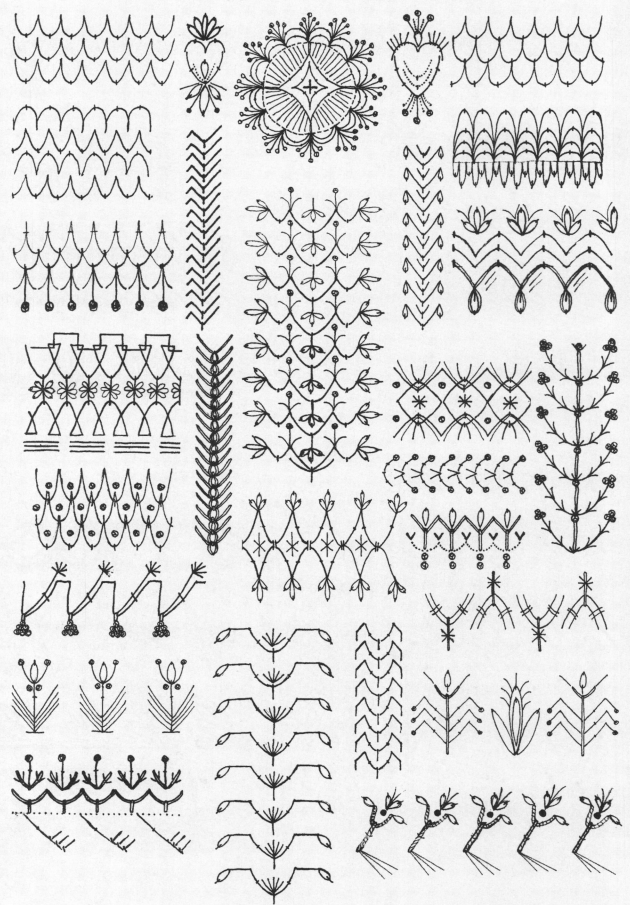

No. 38: feathered chain-stitch designs

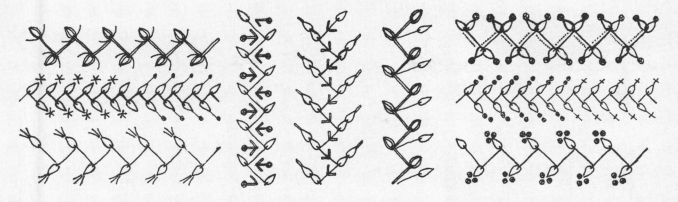

No. 40: closed fly-stitch designs

Detail of original linear chain-stitch design by Mary Lou Sayers

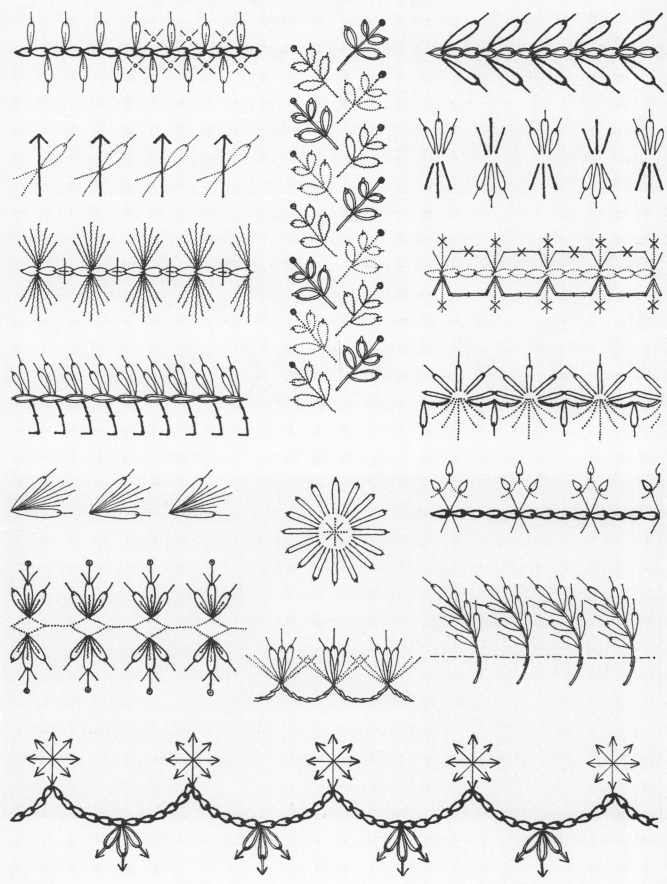

Preliminary drawing of crazyquilt block, by the author, 1998

Chapter Four
Knotted-Stitch & Coiled-Stitch Designs

Detail from "Daddy's Ties Are MOMMY'S Now!", by the author, 1996

The end of the French knot forever: a proclamation (with reservation), and three reasons to master the bullion knot, even though it really is almost as difficult as it looks, at first

There really is a logical reason for proclaiming an old, once-forgotten stitch the rightful, permanent successor to its sometimes imperfect, often obstinate French cousin. I speak of the very well-behaved colonial knot (No. 41), whose appearance is virtually identical to that of the French knot, and whose working method, while more complicated, allows for an almost foolproof result. Colonial knots are also faster to complete. Once you have mastered the easy needle-and-thread twist, you may never again have to experience the dreaded fear of sloppy knots.

Of course, there will always be an exception. The reservation mentioned above is an admittedly biased reference to long-stemmed French knots, also known as pistil stitches, which have become popular and essential among silk ribbon embroidery enthusiasts. You may already know and use these in their most obvious role. I use them, too, but I opted not to include them in this volume because I have never seen one used as a primary stitch on an antique crazyquilt.

The same could be said for stitch No. 42 (see note at bottom of page), the inimitable bullion knot and its companion, the bullion-knot rose. I use these exclusively as embellishers throughout this book. The challenge involved in learning how to make bullion knots lies not so much in the actual procedure as in the lack of information available to us regarding the proper knot-making needles and threads. After three years of struggling to make decent knots using the wrong type of needle, I was fortunate to find a definitive source of instructions: a five-page article in Inspirations Magazine*. The 58 step-by-step color photographs showed exactly where to place the needle and how to hold it. It took longer for me to locate the required package of milliner's needles that I had last used in 1991 than it did to learn the right way to work perfect bullions and roses. I was so happy!

As for my three reasons for mastery of the bullion knot, the first is the beautiful rose that awaits you once the parent knot is learned. The second is the bullion-knot rose buds and leaves used as embellishers on several designs. Last but not least, mastering the bullion knot makes you an automatic intermediate-level needleworker, and that is a very good thing to be!

No. 41: colonial-knot designs

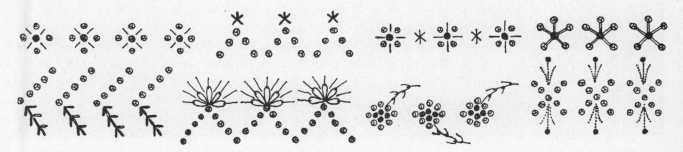

Stitch No. 42 is illustrated in the designs at the bottom of page 159.

Chapter Five

Combination-Technique-Stitch Designs

Detail from "Daddy's Ties Are MOMMY'S Now!", by the author, 1996

Natural selection: the evolution of four simple stitches into 40 fancier forms*

Mariska Karasz called these "composite stitches." They are created in two very different ways. First, at least two stitches, or parts of them, are combined in a way that retains the identity of both, to form a totally new stitch. Second, a separate thread is wrapped around a group of stitches in such a way that the latter is not entirely covered by the wrapping thread. From a list of 14 possibilities, I selected four stitches for this chapter.

Two of these pair the herringbone stitch with a portion of either a cretan stitch to create the cretan-catch stitch (No. 43) or a chevron stitch to make the chevron-catch stitch (No. 44). The fact that both of these are obvious hybrids causes me to believe they were invented and used many, many years ago, but I cannot verify that assumption. The presence of the herringbone-stitch component requires us to work a minimum of two repeats of cretan-catch stitch or chevron-catch stitch as the primary stitch in a linear design. Mirror imaging is also recommended (see the chart on page 71).

A collection of sheaf stitches (No. 45) combines various straight-stitch clusters with one or more wrap-around stitches or with several backstitches, the latter playing an important couching role. Among the nine best variations, (a) through (d) are true antique-quilt stitches, although they were used only infrequently on nineteenth-century crazyquilts. Two others, (e) and (f), are simply the next logical steps in the progression from a three-stitch bundle to a four-stitch and, inevitably, to a five-stitch variation. These are not traditional but look as though they were.

Of the contemporary sheaf stitches, version (i) is the only one I can honestly claim to have invented, if, indeed, it is possible to think of a brand-new, never-before-tried stitch. While all of these are suitable for use as primary stitches in linear designs, simple sheaf stitches in any appropriate size can also embellish other primary stitches, and versions (a), (b), and (c), worked in small sizes, are traditionally seen as open-filling or texturing stitches from time to time.

The butterfly chain stitch (No. 46) is a combination of three uprights and a loop knot, which compresses the cluster of stitches into a sheaf-like bundle. This is another modern creation which gives the impression of an antique stitch, and that alone makes it a perfect choice for crazyquilters. By adding a stitch or two in the same or longer lengths to each bundle, you increase the number of possibilities.

You might find it worth your while to make the acquaintance of the half-chevron/cretan stitch, Guilloche stitch, wheat ear and detached wheat ear stitches, tête de boeuf and tulip stitches, rosette stitch, and even knotted cross stitch. I also loved Joan Waldman's combination of herringbone stitch and double or triple feather stitches. There are more wonderful ornamental composites to be found in the major works of Jacqueline Enthoven and Jo Bucher, should you need additional inspiration.

*the combined number of primary-stitch variations, as shown on pages 50 and 140

No. 43 & 44: cretan-catch-stitch & chevron-catch-stitch designs

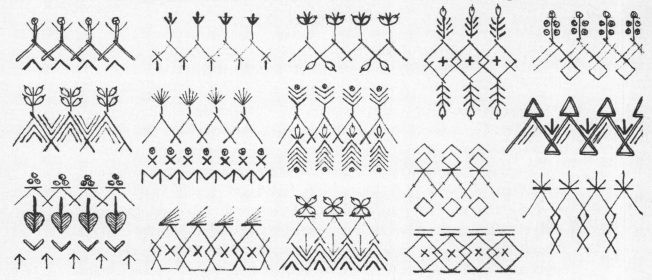

No. 45 & 46: sheaf-stitch & butterfly-chain-stitch designs

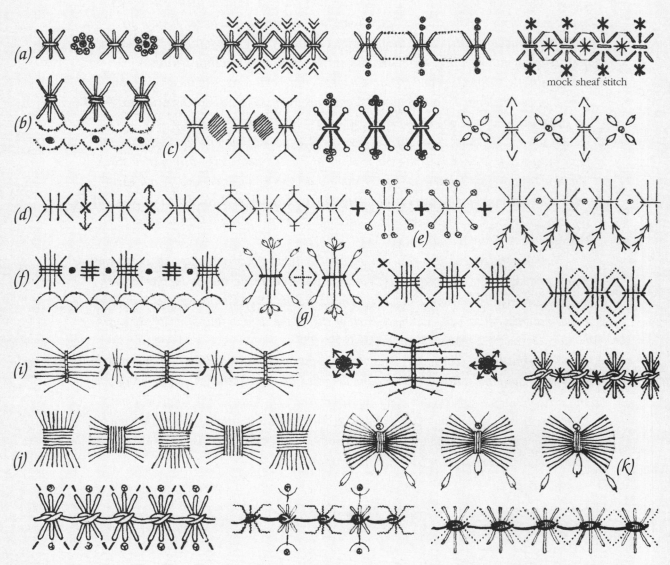

mock sheaf stitch

(a)
(b)
(c)
(d)
(e)
(f)
(g)
(i)
(j)
(K)

Preliminary drawing of crazyquilt block, by the author, 1998

Chapter Six

Laced/Threaded-Stitch & Woven-Stitch Designs

Detail of a crazywork panel, by the author, 1997

More Band Stitches

Both of the primary stitches in Group Six are specialized examples of combination-technique stitches, inasmuch as both require two distinct operations for their formation. Without knowing anything about their origins, I would guess they are perhaps the results of experimental efforts made by at least one advanced-level needle artist searching for a complex-looking linear motif to use as a border. Whether they were created a few decades or hundreds of years ago, neither appears on any of the crazyquilts I have seen.

However, the interlaced band stitch (No. 47) easily earns a place among the traditional stitches by virtue of its being linear and general resemblance to a crazyquilt primary stitch. Not only can this stitch be worked as fancy couching over a narrow ribbon, but there is also no better way to decorate the edges of a stitched or appliquéd bamboo hand screen, a highly ornamental, paddle-shaped fan seen now and then on some of the fanciest antique crazyquilts and on page 177 in this book.

As you study this stitch, you will see that the two rows of backstitches perform the task of anchoring a second, separate thread which is interwoven between the rows (Illus. 6-1 and 6-2). The backstitches are usually equal in length. The stitches in the top row are positioned over the break between the stitches in the bottom row as shown in Illus. 6-4. This important offsetting of both rows of stitches is as difficult as anything I have ever tried to do by eye alone, so pre-marking both linear guidelines to indicate the actual length and starting places of your stitches will help to keep the entire finished stitch as tidy as possible (Illus. 6-5).

couched

Illus. 6-1   Illus. 6-2   Illus. 6-3

Three variations of the interlaced band stitch are presented here. The first, Illus. 6-1, is the one diagrammed and referred to by name in all but one of my source books. I do not work the stitch in the manner shown, lacing the second thread around only one backstitch at a time, because the little loops will close unless they are couched in such a way that they remain open. Illus. 6-2 is my own modification of the original stitch and is preferred because the loops of the weaving thread do not have to be couched in order to keep them from closing. Then, Illus. 6-3 shows an unnamed version which I discovered in one of my old notebooks. This variation is more quickly worked than 6-2, but will use more backstitching thread to cover the same space.

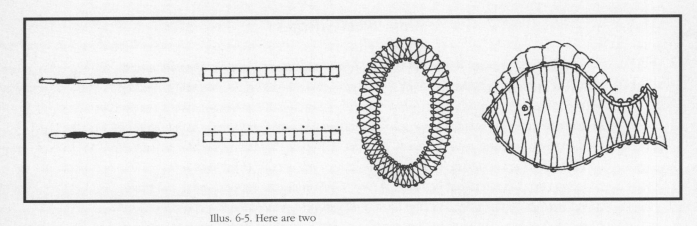

Illus. 6-4

Illus. 6-5. Here are two
pieces of tiger tape for
parallel guidelines.

Illus. 6-6

Illus. 6-7

Interlaced-band-stitch designs can follow a straight or a curved line (Illus. 6-6), and the rows of backstitches, the anchoring stitches, do not have to be parallel to one another (Illus. 6-7). In both cases, all of the backstitches in one design can be worked in any required length to accommodate the proper spacing of the weaving/lacing thread. The fishlike motif shows how an interlacing band stitch can be used as a fill stitch, which makes it a prime candidate for texturing small cloth pieces.

One final thought: You could substitute the double running stitch for the two rows of backstitches in making a length of interlaced band stitch. By doing so, you will be able to use two alternating colors of thread for each row of anchoring stitches. Illus. 6-4 shows how two colors might look.

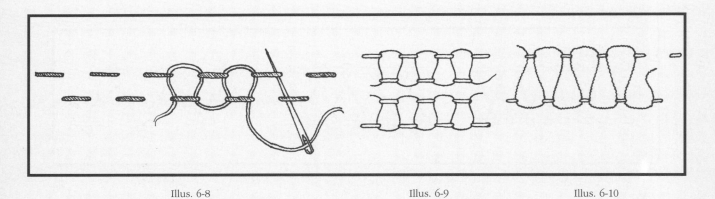

Illus. 6-8

Illus. 6-9

Illus. 6-10

Stitch No. 48, which I prefer to call the laced, stepped double-running stitch (it is called laced, stepped double stitch in the Anchor Manual of Needlework) is another band (i.e., border) stitch, easy to work and old-fashioned-looking. You can couch a ribbon with it or use it to embroider a seam or decorate a portion of a garment or the edge of an enclosed motif. It is also fun to change its appearance in any number of ways (Illus. 6-8, 6-9, and 6-10). Here again, there are a lot of opportunities to use a variety of colors and threads.

The seamwork designs show several variations of both Group Six stitches. In addition, another interlaced band stitch covers the third seam of the fan in the photograph on the next page. I hope you will find these nontraditional stitches worthy of use somewhere on your crazywork project.

No. 47 & 48: interlaced-band-stitch & laced stepped double-running-stitch designs

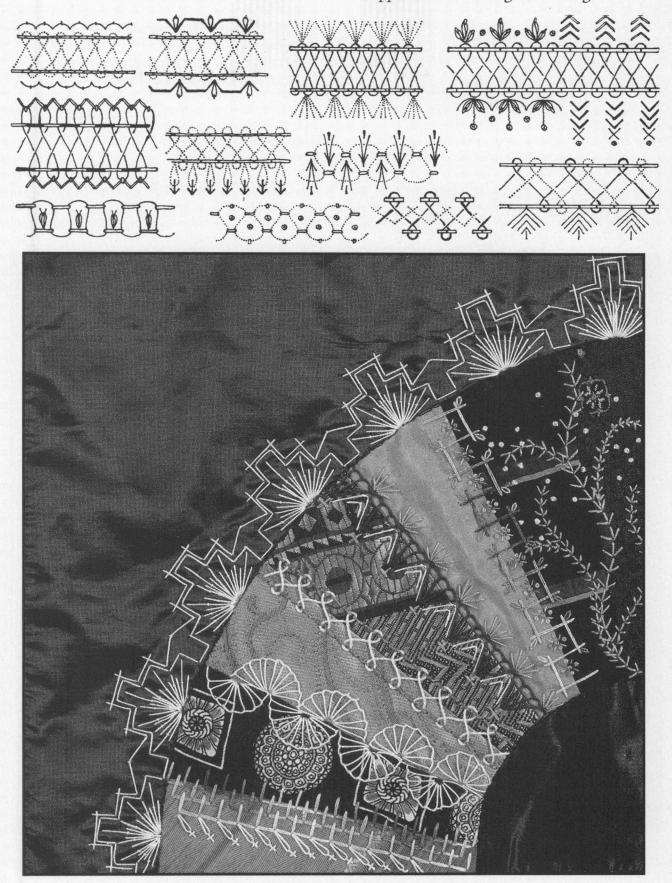

Detail from "Daddy's Ties Are MOMMY'S Now!", by the author, 1996

Chapter Seven
Plain & Fancy Embellishers

Crazyquilt block, by the author, 1993

Stating the obvious:
The more complex the stitcheries, the more beautiful the quilt

As explained in Part One, embellishers are specialized stitcheries that must, by definition, always be a part of another type of embroidered application, whether it be a linear or seamwork design, texturing pattern, or writing. Now that you have encountered so many excellent examples of traditional and original embellishers in the six preceding chapters, I thought you might appreciate having a Catalog of both simple and ornate enhancer stitches and clusters. I hope that, by separating these from their primary stitches, I can help you see how existing stitchery designs can be worked and new ones invented.

The Catalog, pgs. 152 – 159, organizes 800 embellishers into eight different categories based on the most dominant stitch or stitches in each one. Many of these have been documented from dozens of crazyquilts I have studied. Others come directly from *Crazy Quilt Stitches* by Dorothy Bond. Twenty-three were shared by stitchery designer extraordinaire Joan Waldman, and the remainder are designs I created with traditional embellishers in mind. Thousands more variations are possible.

The following observations, while not proposing any rules, should open your eyes to the many ways in which embellishers were used on antique crazyquilts, and at the same time give you a number of guidelines to consider.

How Embellishers Can Be Attached to Their Primary Stitches

Even as they decorate other stitches in the various applications referred to previously, embellishers perform several auxiliary tasks which, though not always obvious, are nonetheless very important to those of us who intend to create our own stitcheries. I have noted six specific kinds of embellishers on this and the next page, followed by 19 positioning options relative to their primary stitches, and I devised a vocabulary of terms to define everything an embellisher can do.

1. INSERTION EMBELLISHERS are either single stitches or clusters of stitches used between two or more detached primary stitches (Illus. 7-1) or inside an enclosed shape formed by repeating linked or connected primaries (Illus. 7-2). Most often, insertion embellishers are centered within the enclosed areas or between primary stitches.
Note: linked and connected primary stitches are not synonymous.

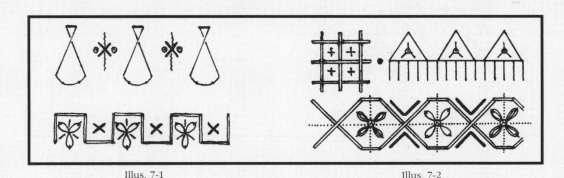

Illus. 7-1   Illus. 7-2

2. COUCHING EMBELLISHERS are stitches used in any decorative way to help anchor any part of another stitch (Illus.7-3).

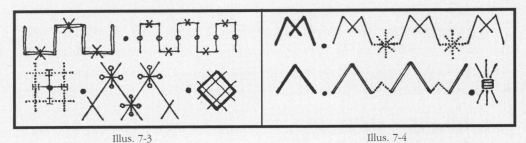

Illus. 7-3   Illus. 7-4

3. CONNECTOR EMBELLISHERS can join two detached, side-by-side primary stitches (Illus. 7-4). The most popular connectors are single straight stitches, detached arrowhead, and cross stitches, but it is possible to get very fancy, as you can see by the illustration. The third design in Illus. 7-4 is a mock sheaf stitch.

4. SHADOWING EMBELLISHERS are worked parallel to any portion of almost any primary stitch, especially a straight-stitch leg or fly-stitch component (Illus. 7-5). Shadowing stitches are most effective when used in the manners shown, in colors different from those chosen for the stitches being duplicated. The shadowing threads can be thinner, too.

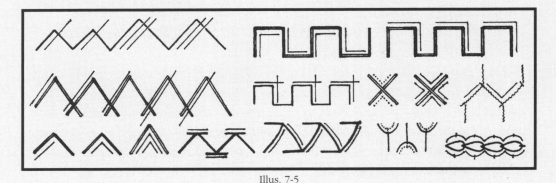

Illus. 7-5

5. ECHOING EMBELLISHERS are actually multiples of a primary-stitch component which repeat that component at regular intervals, or the entire row of primary stitches might lend itself to echo-stitch embellishment. Echoing stitches are always the same size as, or larger than, the primary stitch component being replicated, never smaller. The same color and weight of thread can be used, but contrasting elements are usually preferred (Illus. 7-6).

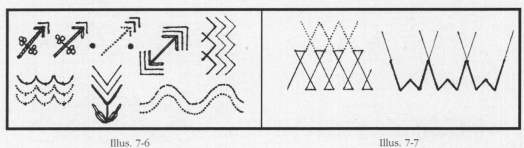

Illus. 7-6   Illus. 7-7

6. EXTENDER EMBELLISHERS (Illus. 7-7) are best worked in lighter-weight threads to lengthen one or more of the straight-stitch components of some primary stitches. This is the most contemporary of the job descriptions I found for embellishers.

The standard placement options for any embellisher are pretty obvious. Simple stitches or a complex combination of stitches can be attached to some part of a primary stitch or detached (floating) somewhere near a component of a primary stitch, or they can be overlaid on each or every other repeat of a primary stitch. Couching embellishers are always overlaid, by definition, while insertion embellishers are almost always detached from their primaries.

Here are several representative examples of the most essential alternatives:

✳ A single stitch or stitch cluster is often centered above or below all the stitches in a seamwork stitchery and can be either detached or attached (Illus. 7-8). The embellishers above the primary stitches can match or differ from those below.

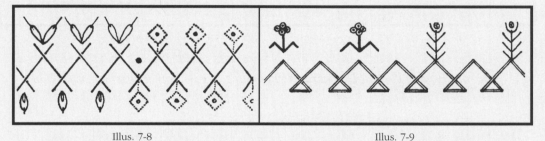

Illus. 7-8   Illus. 7-9

✳ Embellishers can be added to every other repetition of the primary stitch (Illus. 7-9).

✳ Embellishers are also traditionally attached to the ends of certain stitches in a number of ways (Illus. 7-10).

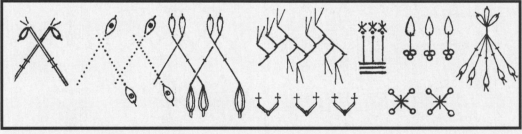

Illus. 7-10

✳ Embellishers, attached or detached, can be added between the intersecting components of some primaries (Illus. 7-11).

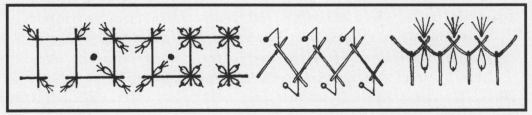

Illus. 7-11

✳ Embellishers can also be added to the long-stitch components of some primary stitches, especially when the latter are free-standing or not closely linked (Illus. 7-12). The decorating stitches can be either attached or detached. Linked-stitch linear embellishers look best when floating parallel to a stitch, as shown in the third example in Illus. 7-12.

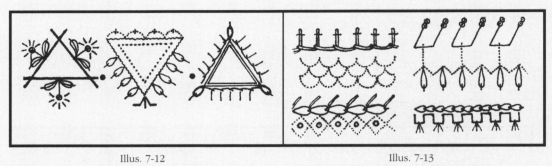

Illus. 7-12   Illus. 7-13

✳ Linked stitches can be worked as one or more rows of embellishers above or beneath a row of linked or detached primary stitches (Illus. 7-13). Note the two attached and two floating examples.

✳ Certain stitches in Group Six can be decorated with embellishers that help to couch or hold the lacing threads in place (Illus. 7-14a). Otherwise, the decorative stitches are usually added in a less utilitarian manner, as shown in both the remaining stitcheries (b).

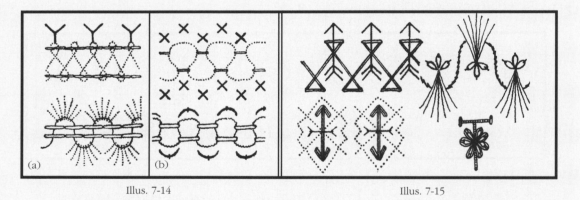

Illus. 7-14   Illus. 7-15

✳ There are at least four special applications for overlaid embellishers. Respectively, an evenly spaced, large-scale, non-linked embellisher can decorate linked and detached primary stitches (Illus. 7-15); detached embellishers can be used to decorate the connector stitches between connected primaries (Illus. 7-16); and large-scale, linked or connected embellishers can be stitched on top of linked or connected primary stitches (illus. 7-17) or on a row of detached primaries (Illus. 7-18).

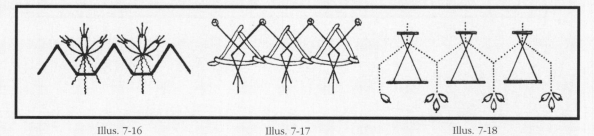

Illus. 7-16   Illus. 7-17   Illus. 7-18

✳ Among less frequently seen placement options, the four stitcheries that follow demonstrate two approaches that require the replication of one element in each design. In Illus. 7-19, a linked (a) or connected (b) embellisher is worked in mirror image above and below a row of detached (a) or connected (b) primary stitches, while Illus. 7-20 shows how the primary stitches are worked in two mirror-imaged, parallel rows with either a connecting row of embellisher stitches (a) or a row of non-connected embellishers (b) inserted between the rows of primaries.

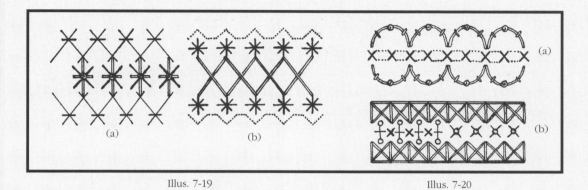

Illus. 7-19   Illus. 7-20

✳ Just as a repeating primary stitch can be worked in the round or in diamond, square, triangle, or oval formation, embellisher stitches are sometimes used to surround an isolated stitchery or small spot motif. Crazy Quilt Stitches contains examples of two very different approaches on pages 30 and 42, while on page 79, feather stitches curve around dainty floral embellishers along a length of chain stitches. My designs are variations on these themes (Illus. 7-21).

Illus. 7-21

✳ Single-stitch embellishers and combinations of stitches have traditionally been used to depict important components of figurative designs on crazyquilts. A colonial knot serves as an eye, a small detached arrowhead stitch suggests a beak, rows of fly stitches become fish scales, and so on. One can also construct buildings with windows, doors, and chimneys, or little rows of churches surmounted with upright cross stitches and synagogues with tiny Stars of David added appropriately.

The Catalog of 800 Embellishers organized into eight categories awaits your pleasure.

Catalog of 800 Embellishers

Straight-stitch-only designs

With enough time and imagination, we could all undoubtedly fill a small book with these embellishers. The 330-plus stitcheries that follow contain from two to 80 individual stitches in each one. They represent only a fraction of the possible configurations, some of them simple, some complex; some borrowed from embroidery designs on antique crazyquilts; and others created by my friends and me, including a lovely assortment of designs from the mind and pen of Joan Waldman.

Of course, we can expand the number of straight-stitch embellishers at least five or six times by adding one or more colonial knots or detached chain stitches, or various combinations of both, to each one. The only limit to our choice of the best embellisher for the job is the amount of time we have to work any design in its entirety.

CQS, 96

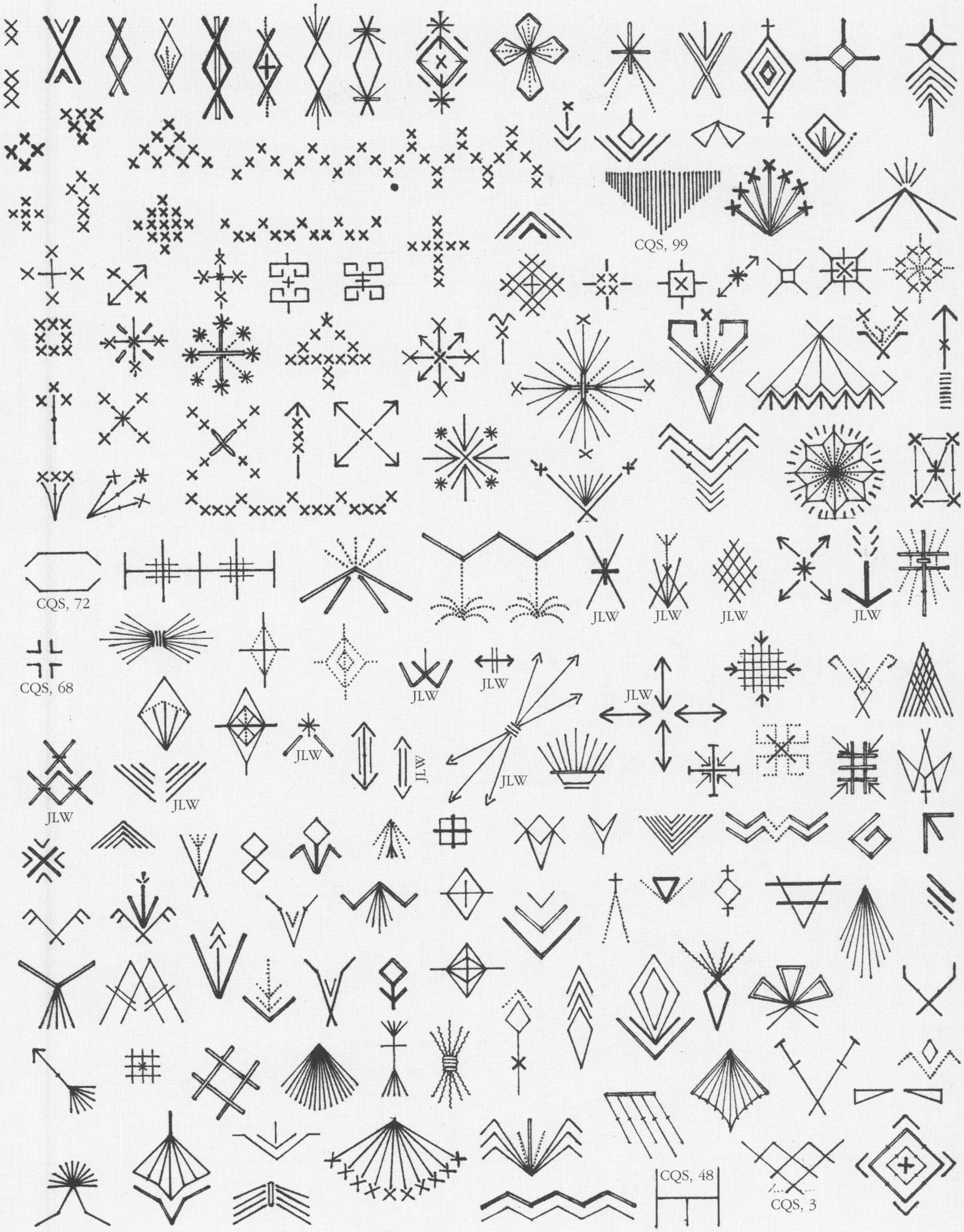
CQS, 99
CQS, 72
JLW
JLW
JLW
JLW
CQS, 68
JLW
JLW
JLW
JLW
JLW
JLW
JLW
JLW
CQS, 48
CQS, 3

Straight-stitch/colonial-knot designs

This next category of embellishers showcases a different selection of stitch formations that were composed by using only basic straight stitches, and with one exception, unclustered colonial knots. Most often, knots were added to one end of a straight or arrow stitch, or knots were centered where two or more straight stitches intersected or were centered or placed, usually one at a time, inside enclosed spaces formed by three or more stitches. I have tried to give you examples of every traditional variation I could find, including six by Joan Waldman which have a definite old look.

In every case, a size 14 (small) or size 11 (medium) seed bead can be substituted for a knot, and you can certainly add more knots to each design than I have.

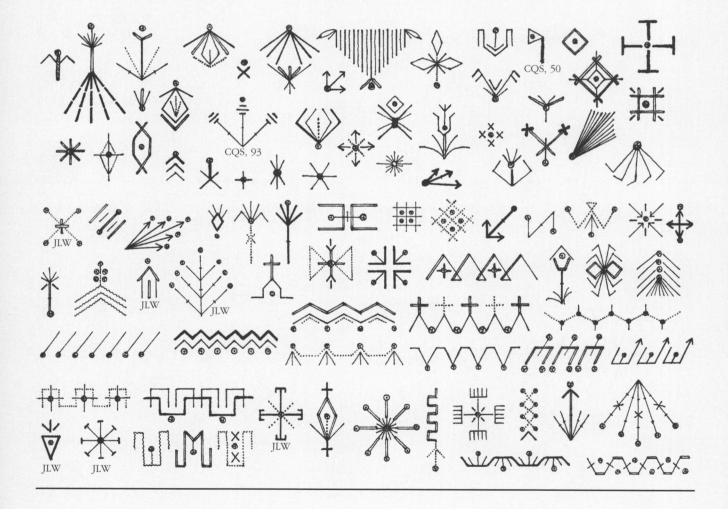

Detached-chain-stitch designs and combinations

Although traditionally, only very simple detached-chain-stitch designs were used as embellishers, they were chosen often enough to make this the second most popular category of embellisher stitcheries. Of course, many of the basic straight-stitch-only clusters, especially the bird's foot, V-stitch, and certain fan clusters, can be worked with detached chain stitches in place of the straight stitches. Thus, we increase the number of designs considerably.

The length and plumpness of each individual detached chain are completely adjustable, and we can vary the number of stitches in any cluster as well. Extra-long or extra-plump stitches should probably be anchored with tiny plain-couching stitches. Whenever a detached chain stitch is large enough, a second, smaller detached chain or straight stitch can be worked inside it in the same or in a contrasting color of thread.

Notice the other variables: tie stitches in any length; multiple tie stitches on one detached chain; colonial or French knots added wherever you like. Two of the clusters are made of double-ended detached chain stitches formed by weaving a teardrop-like loop of thread under the end of each long tie stitch, the loop being the same size as the detached chain itself.

By mixing the types and weights of fibers used in any complex embellisher, even the most commonplace designs will assume added visual importance.

Colonial-knot designs and combinations

Surprisingly, while little knots are used profusely by contemporary crazyquilt makers, they are seen infrequently on antique quilts. In the straight-stitch, straight-stitch/colonial knot, and detached-chain-stitch designs, knots, either French or colonial, usually decorate other embellishers rather than attach themselves directly to primary stitches. It would be hard to imagine the art of decorative embroidery without this important little stitch.

Knots are probably the last embellishers to be added to a complex stitchery. They have tremendous impact when used in clusters. In the following designs, the knots can be worked in the same color and thread as their companion stitches, or both can vary. Except for the three-scallop stitchery, all of these designs can be done with seed beads instead of knots. This may be the most obvious concession we purists must make even as we attempt to be faithful to authentic nineteenth-century modes of embellishment.

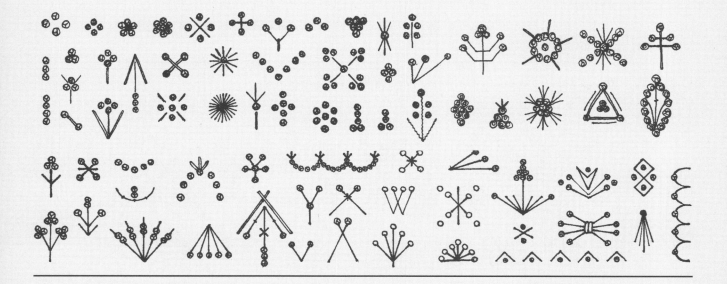

Fly-stitch and closed-fly-stitch designs

We might refer to both stitches as first and second cousins to the basic detached chain stitch inasmuch as their methods of formation are so similar. And yet, as popular and as important as is the detached chain stitch in all its variations, the fly stitch is rarely encountered in embellisher mode on antique crazyquilts. When we do find it, only a simple, unadorned version has been used, as best seen in the designs Dorothy Bond collected. Thus, if today's crazyquilt makers have not discovered the potential these stitches offer, it must be because we have so few antique reference stitcheries in which any of the fly stitches were used.

As you study the designs, notice the nine linear possibilities – those which are repeated side by side along a curved or straight line. Wide-bodied fly stitches, or scallops, would not lie properly without invisible couching to help maintain their special curves. Notice, too, that individual fly stitches may be worked with one or more tie stitches in any desired length (see * in stitch drawings below). There is even a design here in which one fly stitch serves as tie stitches to the two stitches below it (see ** in stitch drawings below). Jacqueline Enthoven gives us permission to replace plain tie stitches with detached chain stitches and with French/colonial knots, one or more per fly stitch. (A note about the first design in the bottom row of this section: In cases where several tiers of fly stitches are stacked and connected to one another in this way, each stitch is completed, one at a time, with the longest row worked first. The drawing gives the impression that all of the stitches are interlocked, but they are not.)

Closed fly stitches, which always fit together as closely as possible, create wonderful leaves with natural veins (centered or not). The feather-tipped arrow provides another embellishment opportunity for which closed fly stitches are the perfect choice.

Satin-stitch designs and combinations

These are occasionally seen on old crazyquilts, but very seldom do they ever embellish the primary stitches in linear stitcheries. I have documented satin-stitch leaves that were attached to double feather stitches. Most satin-stitch work is saved for patch pictures and spot motifs — for flowers, birds, butterflies, and other insects, ships' anchors, and small, solidly filled objects. These are best done using silk thread with a firm twist or flat silk, the most difficult-to-work fiber known to womankind! It is good to keep these embellishers simple to avoid spending too much time on them.

Good to excellent satin stitching requires a lot of patience, practice, a sense of humor, true humility, and more practice!

Combined-stitch designs

All of the 104 stitcheries in this category contain combinations of primary stitches from at least two different embellisher groups. These designs differ from those in the Catalog's second through sixth categories in which only one stitch is dominant. Instead of one dominant stitch in the entire embellisher, there are usually two or three in this category's designs with none of the stitches appearing to be more important than the others. Other, less visually important stitches can be added to the mix, especially unclustered colonial knots and detached chain stitches, a cross stitch, or perhaps small straight stitches. Decorative couching is also an option.

By virtue of their diverse elements, many of these designs are more complex than those already presented. They allow us to get really fancy with our seamwork embroidery, justifying the extra time we must spend to complete them. Even creating such beautiful combinations on paper is extremely satisfying.

Among these stitcheries can sometimes be found elegant figurative designs and others that are so complex we might question their use as embellishers rather than as spot motifs. Of course, we can always decide how best to use any decorative element on our own crazyquilted items. My suggestion would be to work large or intricate pictorial embellishers inside the spaces naturally formed by certain linked primary stitches; or entwine two serpentine lines of chain, stem, or feather stitches and create round or oval-shaped areas in which to place, for example, a butterfly or a vase of flowers. What could be prettier?

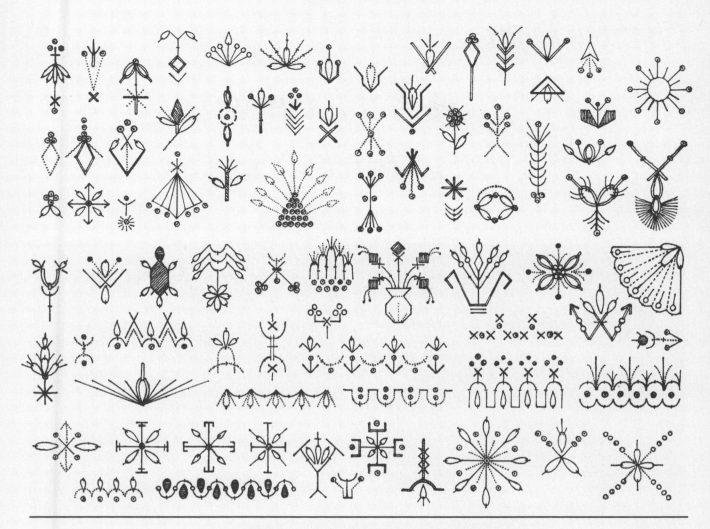

Miscellaneous stitches used in embellishers

A careful study of Crazy Quilt Stitches will reveal 14 additional stitches, the expansion group, which have also been employed as embellishers on antique quilts. Mrs. Bond documented many designs containing blanket, chain, cretan, feather, fern, herringbone, sheaf, stem, and zigzag chain stitches plus bullion knots and four other stitches not selected for inclusion in this book. I offer a few of the stitcheries I created for this category, including a stem-stitch rose and my sheaf-stitch variations. By no means, however, should you consider these or the stitches on this list as your only possible expansion group embellishers.

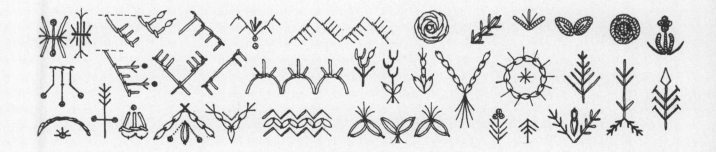

Chapter Eight

Patch Pictures: Music for the Eyes

Embroidered peacock block, a gift to the author from a sister Guild member

Which Stitches Shall We Use?
Choosing the Appropriate Outlining and
Filling Stitches to Create Traditional Patchwork Embroidery Designs

Every serious lover of crazyquilts knows that the most beautiful quilts in this genre always contain the type of embroidery designs I have already described as patch pictures (pages 63 – 65). Without repeating the definitive material from Part One, I offer a close look at the variety of stitches used in the last century to create so many wonderful, often whimsical, motifs.

First, please refer to the Chart on page 57. The column entitled "Decorated Patches" includes all of the outlining stitches and indicates 24 other stitch possibilities for this purpose. The "Fill" column offers an additional group of stitches with which any shape can be drawn, on paper or on fabric, and painted or textured with thread. How these stitches are ultimately used will depend largely on four factors: (a) the type of motif we choose from among the more than 50 different kinds of patch pictures; (b) the degree of realism we wish to portray; (c) the traditional or contemporary nature of the chosen design; and (d) the individual skill level of the quiltmaker.

Fillings are of two basic types: solid, in which no fabric shows beneath the stitches, and open, which more precisely decorate an enclosed area or shape rather than fill it in altogether. Two stitches, satin and Kensington, were the most popular choices for depicting realistic pictures with solid elements. Because the satin stitch is best saved for filling narrow spaces (up to $5/16$ inch or 8 mm maximum recommended width), it works very well on small shapes and in the predetermined sections of complex shapes and free-standing motifs, such as butterfly wings. Much larger areas can be filled with the Kensington or long-and-short stitch, even entire animals, faces, birds, and the like, in addition to the customary leaves and flower petals.

Unless one chooses an over-dyed or variegated thread, the areas filled with satin stitches will be one solid color. The Kensington stitch, on the other hand, is the perfect stitch to use when shadings of color, or a subtle blending of values in one color, are required to give the appearance of dimension to a whole or partial motif. When no shading is needed, the Kensington stitch is simply worked in one color, usually in straight rows.

If you want to diversify the textures in your solid objects and life forms, consider fishbone "leaf" stitch, closed fly stitch, stem stitch, and split stitch to cover any shape completely with thread. The two knots, especially the colonial variety, are less commonly used in this manner but have at least several traditional applications. The remaining stitches in the "Fill" column are excellent decorative fillings. For examples look at the bird's nest on page 170 and the interlaced band-stitch border around the fourth heart design on page 181.

Outlining stitches are necessary for drawing any simple or complex picture or spot motif that will not be completely filled with solid stitches. Of course, open filling stitches can always be embroidered inside outlined areas or shapes. Kate Greenaway pictures, Japanese-style figures and landscape drawings, decorated bamboo hand screens (paddle fans), vases and tea-set pieces, animals of all kinds, and a ubiquitous assortment of religious symbols were among the primary subjects requiring the use of the stem stitch, sometimes in a rainbow array of colors but most often worked in one, high-contrast color against the background fabric, especially white, cream, or yellow thread on black or other dark-colored cloth.

Have you noticed that both stem and chain stitches were occasionally embroidered around satin-stitched shapes to add a hard edge that contains and emphasizes them? This is a perfect way to disguise less-than-perfect satin-stitch work. A further discovery in the details department shows blanket stitches used to outline solidly-filled leaves, with the upright or vertical portions of the stitches pointing away from the leaves to suggest serrated edges.

One final observation: Often, the crazyquilt makers of old elected to represent larger, less complicated, wholly enclosed figures in appliqué form rather than as embroidered images. Thus, horseshoes, hearts, ladies' boots, butterflies, birds, and non-representational objects such as crescent moons with five-pointed stars are found in both formats. Storybook characters, the Greenaway designs, and simple buildings and monuments (and those ever-popular bamboo hand screens) were commonly worked either way. Little flags in full furl were folded or pleated a time or two before being sewn on as dimensional appliqué patches. Most appliqué motifs were embellished with various stitches to make them all the more beautiful and realistic.

For those of you who want to try one or more of the patch-picture designs in this book, here are a few words of explanation. First, several of the antique floral motifs here were traced directly from old crazyquilts. I drew these virtually thread for thread, indicating the actual type and thickness of the threads used in the original designs. The plumpest of these fibers is a fluffy chenille thread. The French knots were done in various sizes of perle cotton as were the stem work and satin stitching. Although in a few places I have given the approximate colors used based on my DMC floss chart, it will be up to you to choose colors and threads (see color illustrations at the front of the book and on page 21).

As I made no attempt to draw any set of designs to scale, I hope you realize that you can also choose to enlarge or reduce the size of any motif. Feel free to change any element of any design to suit your needs. It's a little like substituting ingredients in a recipe to make the dish taste better.

The best thing a serious crazyquilt maker can do is to study as many crazyquilts as possible, both in the cloth and in photographs. If you have not begun your own collection of patch pictures, traditional or otherwise, I hope you will do so, just as you would collect seamwork stitcheries. Sources for stitchable items abound: volumes of an encyclopedia; greeting cards and calendars; wallpapers and borders; costume books; old transfer patterns; red-work quilt-block patterns; mail-order catalogs of all kinds (don't forget the great museum, cross-stitch supply, and gardening supplies catalogs); pretty fabrics, especially paisley, large-scale floral, and figurative prints; cereal boxes; atlases; travel brochures and tourist information materials; computer graphics programs; and even books on various forms of appliqué are natural starting places for designs, not to mention the dozens of books filled with related subject matter. I also love the rubber stamps and découpage pictures currently on the market.

Line drawings are most easily converted into stitcheries. For example, every year, my state income tax information booklet features a wonderful prairie-oriented scenic design on its cover, perfect for rendering in simple outline stitches. I haven't begun to exhaust all the possibilities! Just remember, we must not use copyrighted designs, even when these are not traced directly from a published source, unless the holder of the copyright gives permission. And we should, as a courtesy, seek permission of the owners of the antique quilts which provide the embroidery designs we wish to use, even though technically or legally speaking these designs might be in the public domain or were, perhaps, never subject to copyright law.

Flora Victoriana

Roses, especially the "wild" five-petaled variety, are found on fancy antique crazyquilts too often to count them. Motifs almost always include one or more buds. Lustrous chenille threads, often variegated, were the favorite fiber for embroidery work, but nineteenth-century flower lovers might choose instead to use folded silk or velveteen scraps to create three-dimensional petals and buds.

 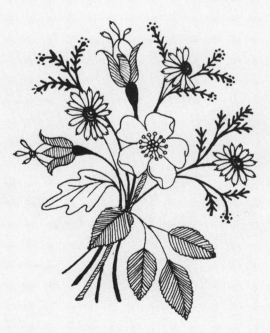

EBR

EBR

KBM

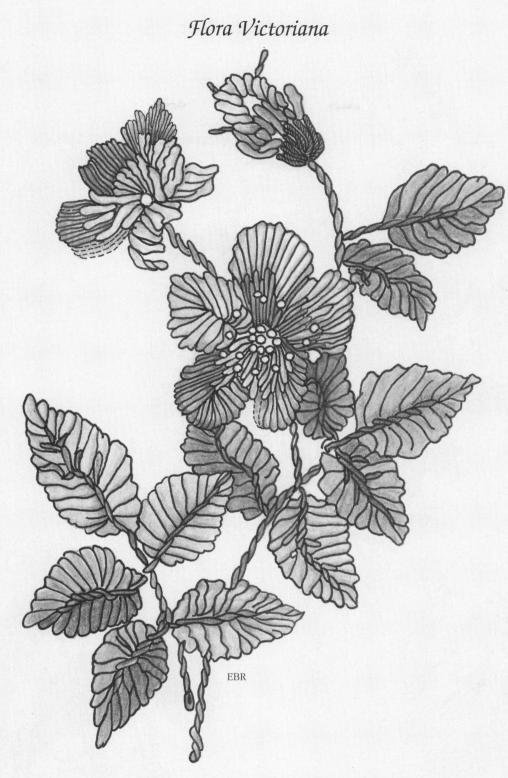

EBR

Wild Roses with Leaves and a Bud

A large floral spray, traced stitch by stitch directly from an antique crazyquilt, is typical of impressive designs that were embroidered in chenille yarns. In this case, three different sizes were used. The stem stitches were done in a thread closely approximating a size 3 perle cotton. It might be possible, and desirable, to work the satin-stitch portions in silk twist in lieu of the hard-to-find chenilles.

Flower Spray with Wheat
& Small Blossoms

EBR

Lily-of-the-Valley Sprig

EBR

Three Strawberries

EBR

Flora Victoriana

Smithsonian
Institution

Two Birds Nesting Amidst Wild Roses

I adapted this wonderful, complex design from a block in the famous Mittie Barrier Crazyquilt, a wool and cotton masterpiece made in 1920. Nine stitches are required: satin (for the eggs, birds, rose petals, and buds); fishbone (leaves); stem; chain stitches; colonial knots; and random cross-hatching (the nest); detached chain (bud tips); blanket (flower centers); and fly stitches (wing and tail-feather tips).

SJ

SJ

Six-Legged Life Forms

No collection of crazyquilt patch decorations would be complete without at least a few insects: beetles and bugs, 'hoppers and flies, bees and skimmers. These individuals are my interpretations of living creatures, suitable for rendering in any combination of stem stitch or backstitch (to outline the bugs and their various body parts), satin stitch, colonial knots, detached chain stitch, and for legs, overcast stitch. Except for the dragonfly and the cricket (second from the left on the bottom row), which could be enlarged, I recommend working each image in the size given. Color coordinate them with your patchwork, if you like!

Human and Angelic Figures

Six people motifs are presented here, a tiny sample of the hundreds of possibilities. Old crazyquilts were more likely to contain embroidered images of children, à la Kate Greenaway or Uncle Remus storybook characters, than adult figures, angelic or otherwise. The prettiest of the stem-stitch outlined designs were worked in several shades of thread: face, hands, arms, feet in one color; hair in another color; clothing and clothing parts in as many colors as the quiltmaker desired. Appliquéing a complex figure gives you the option of adding embellishments to any part of the garments, including laces and other trims in appropriately narrow widths. The long braid on the young girl could actually be created with yarn, floss, or perle cotton threads and invisibly couched in place.

The cloud, left wing, halo, and cap on the standing angelic figure are optional design elements. The right wing can be worked to show all the feather lines, some of them, or none at all.

Kimono must cross left side over right, as shown. Thus, this design is not reversible.

Wearables

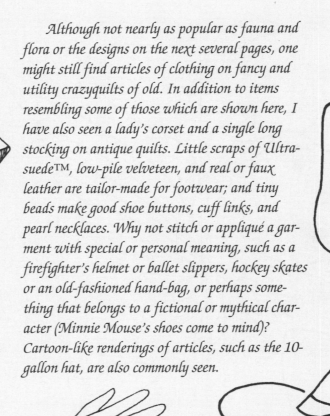

Although not nearly as popular as fauna and flora or the designs on the next several pages, one might still find articles of clothing on fancy and utility crazyquilts of old. In addition to items resembling some of those which are shown here, I have also seen a lady's corset and a single long stocking on antique quilts. Little scraps of Ultrasuede™, low-pile velveteen, and real or faux leather are tailor-made for footwear; and tiny beads make good shoe buttons, cuff links, and pearl necklaces. Why not stitch or appliqué a garment with special or personal meaning, such as a firefighter's helmet or ballet slippers, hockey skates or an old-fashioned hand-bag, or perhaps something that belongs to a fictional or mythical character (Minnie Mouse's shoes come to mind)? Cartoon-like renderings of articles, such as the 10-gallon hat, are also commonly seen.

Bamboo Hand Screens

What pretty things these little fans are! Thanks mostly to the marvelous color photographs in several favorite books, I found 14 traditional shapes for the bodies of the hand screens, although these were usually round or oval. When directly embroidered on a patch, dark fabrics and brightly colored threads were the preferred combination; when worked as appliqués, anything goes, even mixing stitched handles and support ribs with bodies made of cloth. Use beads, laces, and other trims for pretty edgings and to embellish the main areas. The fans may be enlarged up to 400 percent.

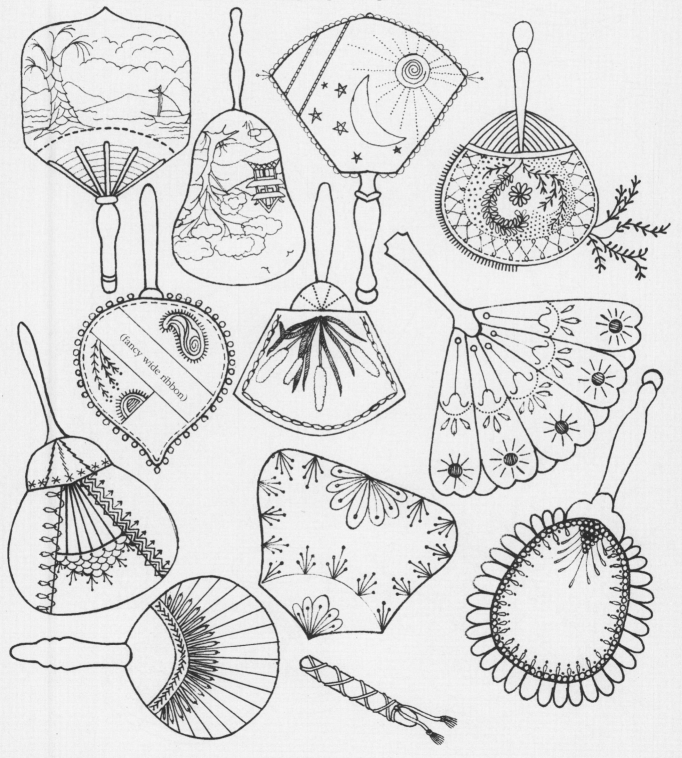

(fancy wide ribbon)

Decorative Porcelain Pieces

These nine designs are meant to be drawn with stem stitches in bright, high-contrast colors on their patches. The large urn (left) was found on four antique quilts. But the delightful little shoe, copied virtually as it appears in life, has sat on a bookshelf for nearly 20 years. It's one of my inexpensive treasures, painted in blues on shiny white.

Valentine/Heart Designs

When my favorite symbol, the heart, is found on old crazyquilts, it appears almost invariably as an appliqué, rarely as a complex or simple stitchery. In fact, I designed all but one of the motifs on this page. Their outer lines can be created with running, stem, chain, blanket, fly, and backstitches, along with colonial knots, interlaced band stitches, and evenly-couched lengths of three or more strands or pieces of thread or yarn. Fishbone "leaf" stitch decorates several hearts.

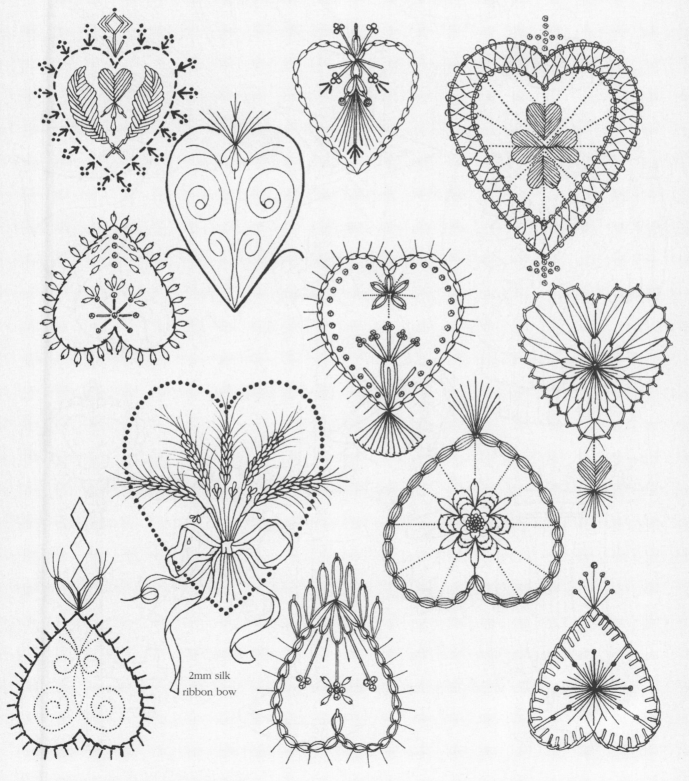

2mm silk
ribbon bow

a painted paper
lantern in one
color on wool

The comet Hale-Bopp (1997) had two tails!

(fill with mixed flowers)

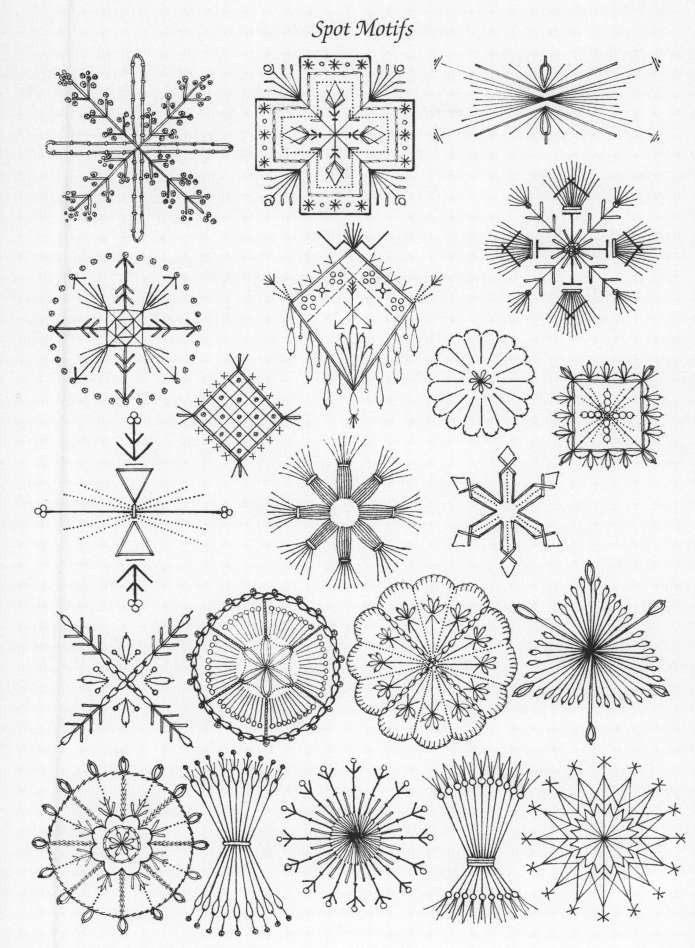

Spot Motifs (continued)

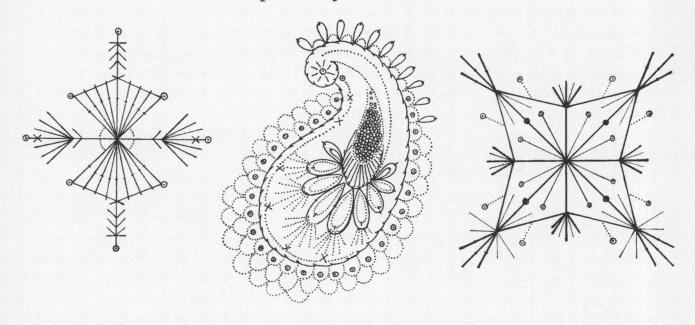

SPECIAL COLLECTIONS: Complex Fan Designs

I have been designing decorative fan stitcheries since 1989 when I saw the design shown first below on an antique crazyquilt belonging to the Museum of American Folk Art. The rest of these are my creations and represent a special form of the complex spot motifs just seen. Whether worked in one color or many, with beads or without, fans never fail to fill an empty space in the most elegant way. Choose among long couched stitches, stem, arrowhead, fly, Holbein, chain, and backstitches to outline, adding detached chain, cross stitch, satin, herringbone, interlaced-band, fly, and long straight stitches plus colonial knots and small stitch clusters to embellish.

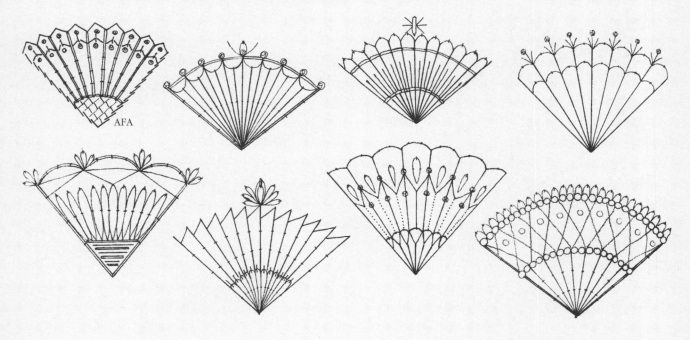

AFA

Chapter Nine

Doodle-Stitch Designs

Crazyquilt block, by Kathleen E. Smith, 1998

Some stitches are just more fun

Not all of the decorative pictures found on antique crazyquilts are as realistic or as complicated as those we have just seen. Over the years, I have collected a small number of simple, mostly whimsical needle-and-thread devices, which resemble the line drawings one might make while thinking about something else – the rather childlike, unself-conscious renderings that Americans refer to as doodling or, more grandly, as non-representational, figurative spot motifs.

Although the cheerful designs in this chapter are actually a specialized form of patch pictures and belong to that stitchery classification, they are distinguished from their more elegant counterparts not only by their apparent simplicity, but also by virtue of the four basic stitches used almost exclusively to create them. The first two stitches, long or short straight stitch and the fly stitch, do all of the outlining. Easy in-and-out stitches form the straight and bent lines, while fly stitches perform an essential role as the curved or scalloped portions of any outline. In both cases, an indispensable technique, plain couching, should be used liberally wherever needed to keep every stitch in its proper place.

I used various detached fly stitches to indicate the head of a small butterfly, the little feet of the turtle, and, in an elongated form, the thorax section of the dragonfly. Three stacked fly stitches masquerade as a pile of stones, while connecting stitches become the edges of a moth's wing, a chick's tail feathers, and the lower edges of the two umbrellas. Do you see how one fairly large, neatly-couched fly stitch can be transformed into a very credible fantasy mouse? Once again, variations on a single stitch are limited only by our imaginations.

Detached chain stitches are perfect for making entire bugs or just their wings and other body parts. The same stitch can be used in a solely decorative capacity, as when I designed the markings for the turtle and the fish's fin. Couch any stitch as many times as required. Use as many tie stitches as you need in any length. Sometimes the legs of a bug can hold a body stitch open.

Having identified doodle-stitch designs as ideally suited for the embroidery of crazy-work patches, I call your attention to the 12 stitcheries that were created especially for seams. You will notice that the individual motifs that comprise each linear design can be identical, as are the tulips, the fences, and the several rows of hearts, or they can all vary somewhat, as do the row houses and tepees. The tulips and hearts can embellish a plain, wide ribbon, too.

Colonial knots, worked singly or in clusters and in threads appropriate to each task, are the obvious stitches of choice for little eyes, for the heads of insects and butterflies, and for small flowers and flower centers, not to mention the pie-dish handle and umbrella handles.

Chapter Ten

Spiders' Webs: A Comprehensive View of a Traditional Motif

Crazyquilt block, by the author, 1995

How to build a spider's web: model homes for eight-legged creatures

Over the years, I have been told three delightful stories, either or all of which may explain why so many crazyquilts contain at least one spider's web among their fancy stitcheries. In fact, after hearing the pious legend of the quick-thinking spider who spun a miraculous web to hide the infant Jesus from Herod's murdering villains, I have felt a little differently about the real-world spiders of my continual acquaintance. I have marveled at the tenacity of my "tenants," building and rebuilding their homes in the out-of-the-way corners of their favorite rooms in my house. I feel guilty nearly every time I dustmop their webs away, and I have finally gotten over being embarrassed when human visitors notice, aloud, that we are not the only living beings in the room.

Like many of you, I am fascinated by these most traditional of all the complex motifs embroidered on nineteenth-century crazyquilts and by the little creatures that inhabit them. But I knew almost nothing about spiders until recently. What I discovered after several trips to the juvenile section of a nearby library both surprised and amused my friends and me. Most importantly, I now know that a spider is not an insect with two extra limbs.

All true spiders have two, not three, main body parts, eight legs, no antennae, and from zero to eight eyes. The legs are attached to the forward part, the cephalothorax. Among the 40,000-plus species of spiders, there is so much remarkable variety in size, color, behavior, and in the type of web any of them may spin that crazyquilt makers can safely take license to create spiders and design webs for our quilts and garments. These are not always easy to stitch well. Spiders especially require a bit of doing to fashion them realistically.

As for the webs, we who stitch them are most likely to concern ourselves with two of the six authentic types my young readers' book described: the orb or cobweb, and the triangle web. (Only members of the family Argiopidae spin orb-shaped webs.) In nature, cobweb makers spin out a silk-like, super-strong dragline and anchor this most essential thread to some object by merely pressing their little spinnerets against something. By an amazing activity known as ballooning, a true spider or spiderling can surf on a breeze to a second location many feet, or even miles, away, and thus start a web virtually anywhere it likes. So, too, without nearly so much excitement or danger, can we.

Embroidered webs often defy nature and the law of gravity, not to mention good design principles, by not being attached to at least a few of the edges of the patches they decorate, or by having concentric instead of spiraling turns, or by having scalloped turns worked in the wrong direction (Illus. 10-1). This may seem a minor detail, but consider: because even their almost immeasurably tiny

Illus. 10-1

weight would naturally cause them to sag ever so slightly, the weaving threads in the bottom half of the web should bend in the same direction as those in the top half, that is, downward. However, regardless of nature or gravity or anything else, if you prefer the traditional look of the web in this drawing, by all means couch your turns accordingly.

Perhaps there exists a proper vocabulary of terms with which we can discuss the various parts of spiders' webs, but since I have not found one, I will use the following words:

Rays are the long threads that radiate from a real or imagined point. All of the rays need not touch that point. In fact, the center or radial point of a web can be off the patch entirely (Illus.10-4 is a perfect example). In nature, the rays in one web can number from 12 to 70, they are not sticky, and they are spun immediately after the anchor threads attach the emerging web to something.

The foundation rays or threads are the two outermost rays in a triangle-style web. Sometimes these are worked in a heavier thread than all the other rays in the same web, but not always (Illus. 10-2).

The anchor threads on crazyquilts are extra stitches which we use to connect the web to the edges of its home patch. A look at the photograph on page 190 will show you how several of the rays were extended to the seams of the six adjoining patches, and how four extra threads, which on this web are not absolutely necessary to its stability, were stitched in a naturalistic way from rays and turns to help strengthen the web.

The turns or weaving threads are the horizontal threads between the rays. In the most natural-looking webs, these will always be worked in the same thread as the rays, but occasionally, you may find a web on an antique quilt in which different threads were used to make the turns and the rays. In such cases, the turns' threads should be finer than the other. Sometimes several turns will be missing (Illus. 10-1 and 10-9). This makes the web far more interesting, in my opinion, than if every thread were intact.

A section of a web is the wedge-shaped space between any two rays, including all the turns therein. As each spider has its own aesthetic, its web will reflect its preference for near-perfect symmetry or for an asymmetrical design. Thus, many spiders (and some crazyquilt artisans) build webs with every section equal in width; but a strong dislike for rigid symmetry dictates the choice of a freer, more organic style of web building with obvious irregularities worked intentionally into each one (Illus. 10-6, 10-8, and 10-9).

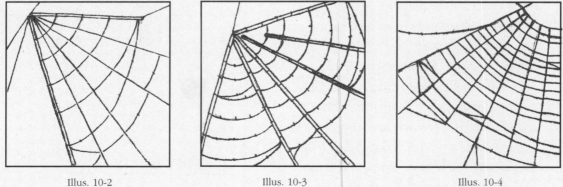

Illus. 10-2   Illus. 10-3   Illus. 10-4

The Various Architectures of Spiders' Webs

In the most general sense, all webs found on crazyquilts are based on two primary structures: the wheel and the fan. Beyond this, there are several basic formations we can choose when stitching a web, and here I am necessarily limiting myself to a discussion of the biologically correct cobweb and triangle types, as mentioned earlier.

A. The full-circle web. These roundish, wheel-based structures are the most common form found on antique crazyquilts. Rarely will you find one that resembles a true circle, however, and this is just as it should be, since spiders do not build perfectly circular homes in real life.

On cloth, full-circle webs can be presented in a number of formations which are neat and regular, with equally spaced rays and turns, and which are based on either a hexagon, an octagon, or a fairly evenly divided wheel (Illus. 10-7). So, also, can an irregular or untidy-looking web be constructed within a circular outline, this time with unequal spacing between rays and between weaving threads (Illus. 10-5, 10-6, and 10-8).

By the way, there is a wonderful example of an octagon-based web on the cover of Crazy Quilts, with an enlarged view on page 58. In this house must surely live one very compulsive-obsessive creature! I can imagine her, using a protractor and engineer's ruler to get every thread so straight and even. As beautiful as it is in its perfect symmetry however, its design seems only to suggest a dwelling place for a spider, rather than to represent an actual web. (If this one appeals to you, practice your backstitching!)

Illus. 10-5   Illus. 10-6   Illus. 10-7   Illus. 10-8

B. The quarter-circle web. These are, of course, fan-based. As the name indicates, each web is a portion of a circle (and the latter may be truly round or nearly so), with the foundation rays stitched perpendicular or almost perpendicular to each other. These two threads thus form an approximate 90-degree angle at the convergence point (Illus. 10-9).

If you want to create as realistic a web as possible, the foundation rays should anchor the web to the edges of the patch you are working on. All the other rays radiate straight out from the convergence point, although not every ray actually touches the center of the web, as you can see in Illus. 10-3, 10-4, and 10-8.

It is a good idea for both foundation rays to be about the same length, but the interior rays can be any reasonable and pleasing length, whether equal or unequal to each other, or whether longer or shorter than the foundation rays (Illus. 10-2, 10-3, 10-4, and 10-9).

Can you see that the web shown in Illus. 10-9 is not true to nature? Four of the interior rays end in mid air, and this simply would not occur in reality. If I were to extend those four short rays until they touched the ribbon, and if I added more weaving threads, this web would be fairly true to life. Or I could add one line connecting the long interior rays (A to B), extend the two short rays to touch it, and create an even more natural-looking web.

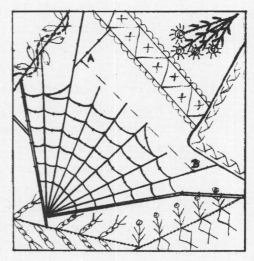

Illus. 10-9

C. The less-than-90-degree web. The name says it all. These are very triangular in shape and fit easily into accommodating acute angles on some patches. I have not yet encountered such a structure in person, but I trust the book that described and showed pictures of the six generic web forms, one of which was not unlike the one I drew for Illus. 10-13.

I noticed in close-up photos of Ms. Montano's work that her "Type-C" webs sometimes have as few as three rays (nicely spaced). There is no rule, but you will probably find that these narrower webs display more regularity than do the other types; and they rarely have any additional attaching threads to secure them to their patches, allowing their longest rays to perform that task (Illus. 10-11, 10-12, and 10-13).

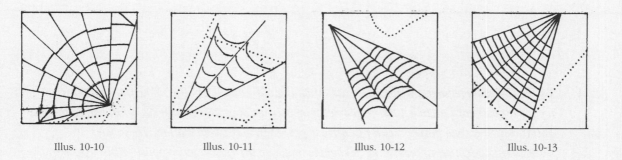

Illus. 10-10   Illus. 10-11   Illus. 10-12   Illus. 10-13

D. The 100-degree-to-180-degree web. These webs resemble an expanded fan, one which opens no farther than its full span, that is to say, up to a half circle, and which is wider than 95 degrees at its convergence angle. These biologically incorrect webs can be quite showy and are a very good alternative to a full-circle web (Illus.10-3 and 10-10).

A Matter of Style

Inevitably, every serious crazyquilt maker will develop her own style of embroidered spider's web. I like to think of these as either left-brained or right-brained creations and, thus, as true reflections of the human artists' personalities. After many trips outside to study orb-shaped webs, I realized that there isn't a lot of structural difference between one real web and another, even when these are made by different spiders. The tenant spider who lives in our juniper bushes, for example, chews out her webs' centers, while the occupant of the gorgeous, eye-level home attached to our house and one clothesline in the rear keeps the centers intact, spinning a few rounds, then leaving a space approximately three-quarters of an inch wide all around, and then finishing the web. She makes the most exquisite anchoring brackets, and she even has an auxiliary web, a garage, perhaps, or a tangled spider gazebo, upon which she perches waiting for … company!

To come closer to the point, hand-worked webs can vary in several noticeable ways. These elementary differences pertain more to style than structure and are plainly analogous to individual variations in hand-writing styles among several people. Each of us will make certain choices that will ensure the uniqueness of our creations. The most important style factors are as follows:

The type of thread used to make the web. We have multi-strand flosses in cotton, silk, and rayon; twisted threads, including all the perle cottons, linen, and flower thread; filament silks, and metallic threads, for starters. The same web could conceivably be worked in dozens of different fibers. Of course, no self-respecting spider would ever spin the same web twice.

The number of strands of floss used in various parts of the web.

The color and the value (lightness or darkness) of the thread. Just as a limited number of fibers will produce a more natural-looking web than all the others we could choose, so also, do a handful of colors seem better suited to that end. Of course, to be as realistic as possible, we would have to use clear, monofilament nylon thread all the time, wouldn't we? Still, absolutely any color can be used to stitch a spider's web, and the color selected can either be of high-contrasting or low-contrasting value against the background patches. I suspect most of us would pick fibers, colors, and values that best ensure the visibility of these time-consuming motifs, at least most of the time.

The stitch or stitches used. Crazyquilt webs are traditionally worked in long straight (laid) stitches, stem stitches (the most commonly found), backstitches, tiny chain stitches (infrequently), and/or fly stitches in a number of logical combinations. I prefer the overall look of long-stitch and fly-stitch webs in spite of the fact that they take a long time to couch nicely. You may find that stem stitching gives you the best control when the rays and weaving threads are very straight.

All that remains is to spin the web of your dreams – a fitting dwelling place for the spider in you!

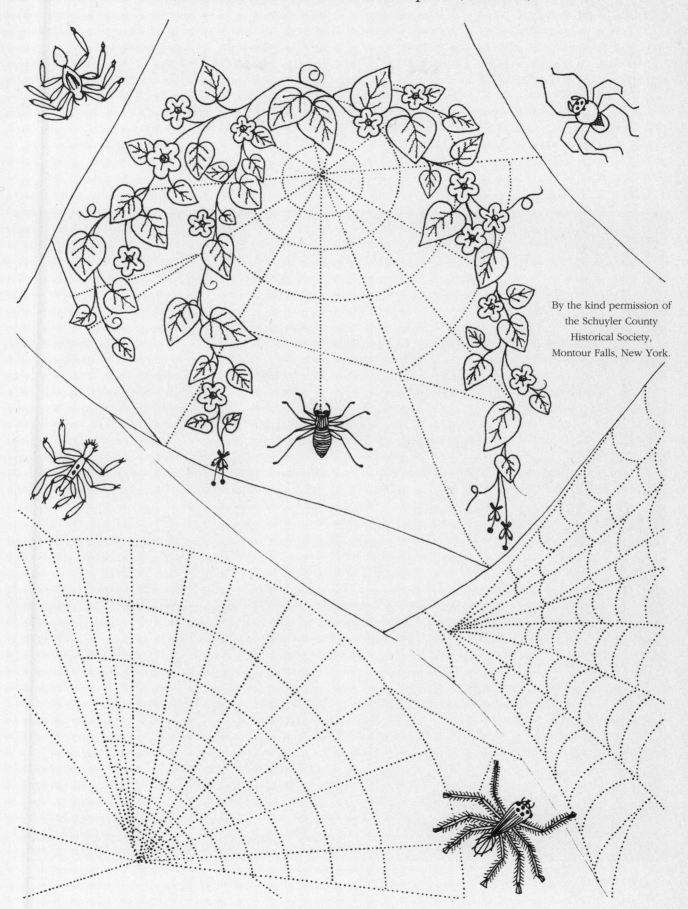

By the kind permission of
the Schuyler County
Historical Society,
Montour Falls, New York.

Chapter Eleven
Alphabets & Words: Embroidered Writing

Crazyquilt block, Betty Pillsbury, 1998

To make each quilt your own…

The fourth category of special stitchery is writing. Very few contemporary English or American embroidery books give much space to the subject of handwriting worked in stitches. Surely this was not the case a hundred years ago, when, I imagine, our grand-mothers and great-aunts must have monogrammed just about everything they could put a needle into. Much excellent instruction in proper techniques would have been necessary to guarantee no less than admirable results in those well-brought-up ladies' efforts to label their wearable belongings and the crazyquilts they made with their own names or fancy initials.

Antique crazyquilts of the elegant variety employed a number of traditional alpha-bets for autographing and dating them. Among the most popular of these was the Gothic or Old English style. The letters were large enough to be formed in satin stitches with broad-to-narrow stem stitches for the tapering portions or flourishes of each letter. Over-cast or trailing stitches were used for the solid bars found on many of the capitals.

Needless to say, this is not the easiest alphabet to master. You will also find that there are more than 100 different sets of true Gothic letters, with distinctive ways to ren-der several of the capitals, especially the G, H, I, J, N, O, Q, T, and Z. The variant form that I have chosen to include in this chapter is one of the more complex, but anyone who possesses intermediate-level hand-embroidery skills will have no trouble working the let-ters of your choice. You should use a fine silk buttonhole twist or soie perlée, or two strands of high-quality cotton floss or silk floss, following the pre-drawn directional lines, if you like, and without further embellishment.

Another old-fashioned alphabet found on numerous crazyquilts is represented on page 202 by three fancy letters: A, C, and H. These letters show a pretty variation of the com-mon Gothic or Old English form, and it would not surprise me if it took six hours or more to work each letter. The primary aspects of each one are two narrow bands of satin stitch-es, not padded, with a space between the bands. These spaces usually contain a single row of evenly spaced colonial knots. This style of lettering also uses one or more lines of stem stitches to replace at least one of the vertical elements in many of the capitals. As you can see, the H does not have a stem-stitch support line. The three named stitches that form an actual letter are always worked in one color, not three, while the little floral motifs attached to the letters are invariably multi-colored.

I traced the three examples of this unnamed alphabet directly from the quilt they were stitched on, closely following the directional stitching lines to help you see how each letter might be reproduced. Lustrous perle cotton thread, size 5 or its equivalent, was used except for the five-petal, detached-chain-stitch blossoms, which appeared to be done in the tiniest possible chenille thread.

Pages 206 and 207 show another great alphabet for writing on crazyquilts which is wonderfully feminine even without floral adornment. This classic italics style can be accomplished in three different ways (see Illus. 11-1): by the use of satin stitches for solid filling of the letters; by using stem stitches to render the letters as either two-dimensional motifs (much like real handwriting); or as letters with not only width and height but visual thickness, as well, and with both broad and narrow "trailing" aspects. One such ornamental version of italic-style lettering can be seen spelling "Grace" on the magnificent Tamar North Crazyquilt, one of the most beautiful quilts ever made. The letters themselves are white, and the little flowers are blue with yellow centers and green foliage.

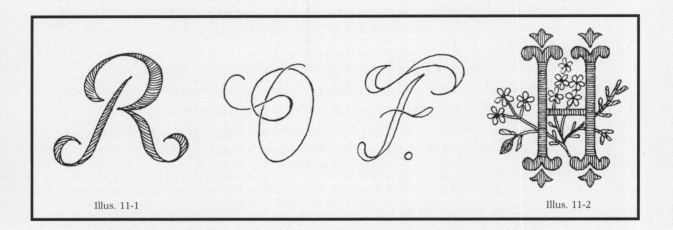

Illus. 11-1

Illus. 11-2

As I wrote the first draft of this chapter, I opened the award-winning book, Nebraska Quilts & Quiltmakers, to page 151 and spent a few moments studying an interesting set of initials with my magnifying lens. Actually, that particular friendship or fund-raising quilt, now in the collection of the Nebraska State Historical Society Museum in Lincoln, is loaded with names, towns and cities, and the date of its completion, all embroidered in satin-stitched Gothic letters in many colors. (Illus. 11-2 shows one of the monogram capitals I like so well.) It is probable that nineteenth-century needle artists chose their flower-sprigged initials from one or more popular publications of the time, and they obviously enjoyed a challenge.

Not all of the writing on crazyquilts was fancy to look at or difficult to stitch. Very often, the quiltmaker decided on simple, stem-stitched words and names without additional embellishers. Backstitches in one row or in two to three rows worked very close together might accomplish this task, or the maker might prefer chain-stitched script. She might also have traveled back a hundred years or more in time to retrieve a plain or a gorgeous cross-stitch alphabet, or she could have put her talents to a wholesome and proper use by creating her own original lettering style. If she was really good, she might even design a multi-use monogram with one letter superimposed on or interwoven with another. Regardless of their simplicity or complexity, every letter can be decorated with a traditional or contemporary assortment of small designs and stitches.

You and I could reasonably be expected to inscribe our patchwork with meaningful modern phrases, such as (please forgive me): "Elvis Lives!" or "The Right Stuff" or "Live Long and Prosper!" Pieties can be given special importance by enclosing them inside fancy frames, also know as cartouches. An excellent example of this application would be to stitch the word "Love" inside a beautiful heart shape, perhaps an enlargement of one of the designs on page 181. Of course, names and dates can be treated in the same way.

I hope you will decide to sign and date your crazyquilts on the front, either quietly and unobtrusively or boldly enough to be seen from 10 yards away. If you choose one of the formal, antique-style alphabets for your words and messages, you will need to master the satin stitch and the overcast stitch first. As I explained in Part One, perfect satin stitching requires a good foundation, and I have had almost instant success by outlining the main parts of each letter with split stitches (Illus. 11-3) and then filling in the enclosed areas thus formed with little, loose seed stitches (Illus. 11-4). Satin stitches are worked across the main portions of the letters, perpendicular to the outlining stitches or at a slight diagonal to the true horizontal line of each separate part of a multi-sectional letter. Every part of any complex letter, such as those shown, will usually suggest an appropriate slant or orientation for the satin stitches. However, there really is no rule about the most proper direction for working them. When in doubt, simply do what you think will look best. You can even sketch your desired letters and draw mock satin stitches to indicate various possibilities for completing the motifs. Illus. 11-5 shows just such a preliminary sketch with the satin stitches worked in two different directions, (a) and (b).

Because Treasury of Crazyquilt Stitches is about traditional techniques, I have not

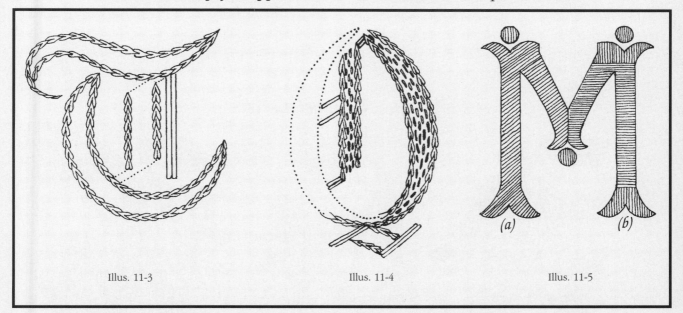

Illus. 11-3   Illus. 11-4   Illus. 11-5

offered suggestions for letters and words formed in any way other than with needle and thread and standard stitches. Many alternatives for writing on quilts do exist, however, including making appliqué letters and manipulating ribbons to create monograms and the like. In fact, anything that can be couched onto the patchwork becomes a candidate for this purpose, whether narrow or wide ribbons (single, stacked, braided, twisted, ruched, or scrunched), lace trimmings, beads of every kind, sequins (pre-strung or individual pieces), rows of buttons or jewels, cordings, or even shoestrings made of cloth or leather. Both the appliquéing and the couching stitches can be practically invisible, or they can be as decorative as you want.

Among the very best sources of lettering styles and framing motifs are the many

Dover Publication books that contain ornate names and stitchable monogram initials and should supply any crazyquilt maker with sufficient material to use for a long time. Old embroidery transfers designed for the embellishment of pillow cases and other fancy linens are also helpful and available at large discount craft-supply stores. Look for *Inspirations* and *Sew Beautiful* magazines, and anything written by Mary Jo Hiney. Collect the decorative capitals that are used as the first letters in the opening text in each chapter of many excellent books. One of my favorites is the *Woman's Day Book of American Needlework* by Rose Wilder Lane, but there are hundreds to choose from, if you will only take the time to search for them.

My final recommendation: practice your embroidered writing on something less important first. Experiment with the various fibers you have on hand, and discover the unique and occasionally unpredictable properties of each kind of thread. Once you have confidence in your stitches and know what your threads can do, you will surely find just the right place for that impressive monogram you've been dying to try!

Pious Words: Satin/Stem-stitched Script, Original Design

Antique Alphabet Letters

Traced from an antique crazyquilt, circa 1885, owned by Elizabeth Reinig, Panama, IA

Love Joy Hope Charity ihs Faith

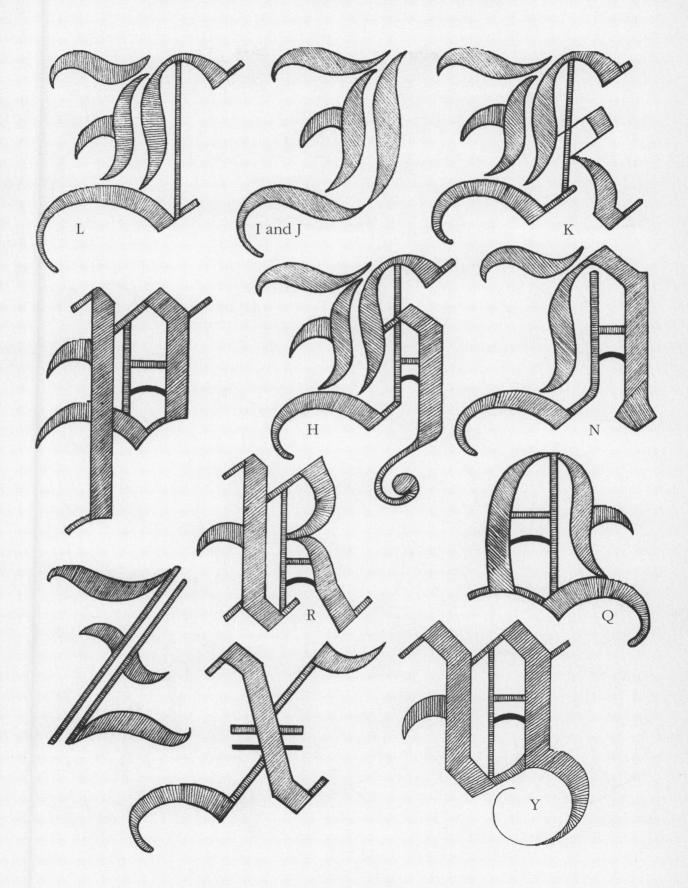

reverse S to make
an ampersand

Chapter Twelve

Texturing

Crazyquilt block, Mary Lou Sayers, 1997

Detailing the Details . . .

We come to the last chapter in the *Treasury of Crazyquilt Stitches*. *Texturing designs* comprise the fifth category of special stitcheries in which we use thread to embroider our fancywork items. Although only occasionally seen on antique crazyquilts, these sometimes predictable, always interesting patterns were used often enough to warrant a closer look.

Texturings are specialized embellishers. They do exactly what their name implies: they add an extra tactile and visual dimension or texture to the patches of cloth they decorate. There are at least 12 distinct design possibilities, whose methods I describe for you on this and the next four pages, for texturing our fabric, but you should know that most of the examples I found on old quilts are worked according to Methods 4 and 5 described on page 210.

Perhaps the most important thing to keep in mind is the fact that only two generic forms of texturing exist: the embroidery stitches will either depend in some way upon a printed motif or woven pattern on the patch, or the added stitching will not be based on anything which may appear on the patch being embellished. Obviously, this second broad category of texturing designs will be most often, although not exclusively, used to decorate solid-colored, plain-woven fabrics.

Here, then, are a few excellent ideas for making your crazywork even more beautiful, if, indeed that is possible. In addition to the graphic illustrations provided for this chapter, several of the photographs in the book contain texturings on a patch or two. Try to imagine and draft as many variations of each of the following methods as you can, always remembering that the final effect of your labors will have much to do with your choices of thread types, colors, contrast in values, and everything else we have discussed.

1. Any printed or woven motif on the cloth may be outlined by certain embroidery stitches (please refer again to the Chart on page 57). For example, one might stem-stitch or backstitch around a leaf, a tea cup, an animal, a flower and its individual petals, or another motif one wishes to emphasize. But there is more.

2. Any printed or woven motif on a fabric may be filled (completely or partially) or accented in some natural way with stitches. If the aforementioned leaf has vein lines, these can be enhanced. The flower's center might present the perfect place for a cluster of colonial knots, and the tea cup could be further embellished with all manner of pretty stitches which would exactly follow its printed design. Self-contained paisley motifs, which can be embroidered in place or cut out and appliquéd to a plainer piece of cloth, are among the best candidates for Methods 1 and 2. Satin stitches, fishbone stitch, or closed fly stitch can entirely fill small contained shapes such as circles, squares, hearts, leaves, and the like.

3. Certain motifs on printed cloth are designed to closely resemble or even duplicate embroidery stitches. I am thinking of a delightful Christmas print I purchased in 1975 which features cross-stitch figures reminiscent of old-fashioned sampler spot motifs. By selecting identical colors and just the right threads, a subtle dimensional element could be added. Do you remember the crazy-patchwork "cheater cloth" that was so popular in the mid-1990s? All the stitcheries printed on it simply begged to be rendered in thread; in fact, several friends and students of mine used this very fabric to practice their crazyquilt-embroidery skills. Method 3 is limited to the sort of fabrics I described, making this one of the rarest of all the texturing forms.

4. Any straight line, geometric pattern, be it a gingham, a plaid (even or uneven), a checked print, an overall grid of intersecting lines, or a checkerboard-like design, can be embroidered with long, laid stitches or back stitches, running stitches, stem stitches, or any combination of these outlining stitches in such a way that the geometric nature of the pattern is defined. The laid stitches can be plain couched along their length, if necessary — usually at regular intervals; but at the very least, fasten long threads to the fabric and to each other wherever the threads intersect. (Cross stitches and colonial knots or small seed beads will perform this task very nicely.)

5. Instead of stitching upon the various lines on patterned cloth, whether to create a grid exactly as it appears or to draw attention to the places where one color ends and another begins, the spaces between grid pattern lines as well as the alternating and repeating blocks of color which are inherent in ginghams, checks, and plaids can also be decorated. The truth is, nineteenth-century crazyquilters were most likely to choose gingham or a fabric with a simple pattern of crossing lines to embellish with petite texturing stitches. The larger areas of color found within most plaids were and are perfect places to embroider spot motifs and doodle-stitch designs in appropriate sizes. The quiltmakers of old rarely spent much time on these stitcheries, but seemed to be interested in prettying the commoner scrap-bag patches as quickly as they could.

Did you think I had forgotten about stripes? Well, I almost did! It seems so apparent that we would use Methods 4 and 5 to add a wonderful variety of stitcheries to striped fabrics, although other texturing possibilities do exist. I have personally seen only one quilt on which this was done, with a seamwork design embroidered inside the wider, lighter-valued bands of a two-color, uneven stripe. The effect was definitely that of several fancy-couched ribbons stitched onto a darker piece of cloth at regular intervals. When all of the stripes are narrow, the stitches should be simpler, whether linked, connected, or detached.

6. Relatively simple or very complex texturing designs can be created on solid-colored cloth (with or without woven or embossed features). As lovers and practitioners of crewel embroidery are well aware, even small shapes (such as a leaf or petal or calyx) which comprise a larger motif can be textured with laid threads/yarns, couched where they intersect, with optional tiny stitches or stitch clusters worked in the spaces between the laid threads. For our purposes, we could just as easily employ a combination of Methods 4 and 5 to enhance an entire patch, except that we would be stitching on unpatterned fabric. I especially like the idea of doing this on velvet or velveteen. Experiment with fancy threads, narrow cording, even sequins and beads for a contemporary, sparkling effect. Several examples are offered in Illus. 12-1(a).

7. Any fabric, whether it be solid in color or whether its overall pattern be printed, woven or embossed, can be textured with the following stitcheries: Illus. 12-1(b) one stitch or stitch cluster, detached and repeated at regular, evenly-spaced intervals; Illus. 12-1(c) one stitch or stitch cluster, not touching each other, but randomly scattered on the patch; Illus. 12-1(d) two or more simple stitches or stitch clusters, detached, alternating in a uniform pattern; and not shown, two or more stitches/stitch clusters, detached and repeated in an irregular pattern on the cloth.

    Stars and snowflakes in their many varieties, detached-chain-stitch flowers and other motifs, cross stitches, single or clustered colonial knots, sheaf-stitch bundles, and even stem-stitch spirals are among the best choices for this method of embellishment. The individual stitches and clusters may be worked in any desired sizes, while the patterns as a whole need not conform to any printed or woven design on the cloth. Having said that, it makes a lot of sense to use any simple, repeated (printed or woven) motifs on a piece of cloth in the most obvious way: namely, to help us determine exactly where to put the stitches. I recommend that you apply Method 7 to a polka-dotted or star-print fabric, if you have one, and that you search through your necktie collection for a suitable foulard or for pieces which contain all-over patterns of small, evenly-spaced designs (see Illus. 12-2 for additional designs).

Illus. 12-1(a) Illus. 12-1(b)

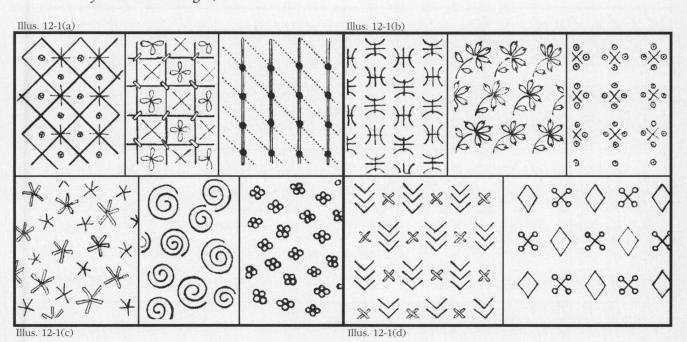

Illus. 12-1(c) Illus. 12-1(d)

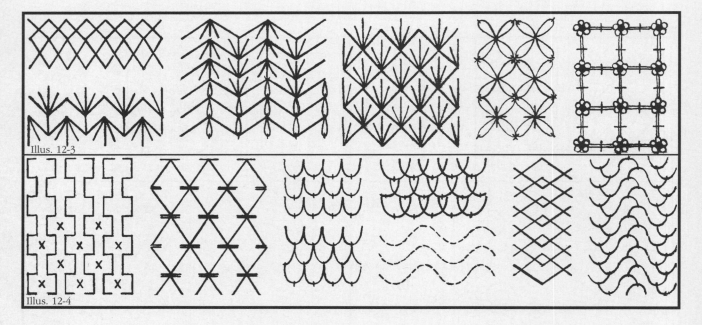

8. One stitch or stitch cluster can be repeated in such a regular manner that it forms a decorative grid-like design on the fabric. The individual stitches/clusters always touch each other somewhere along a row, and rows of stitches either connect or are not attached. If detached, the rows are always evenly spaced, fairly close together, and may be worked horizontally, vertically, or diagonally, as desired. If more than one repeating stitch is used, one of them is usually dominant in the overall pattern (Illus. 12-3).

9. In an obviously similar approach, any of the linking and connecting stitches as well as other non-enclosed stitches which can be interlinked along a line can also be selected to texture fabric. Again, rows of stitches may or may not touch each other. All of the basic herringbone, blanket, feather, and cretan stitches are recommended for this application, as are most of the chain stitches, fly stitches, arrowhead and chevron stitches, and the Holbeins (Illus. 12-4). Rows of stitches (using Method 8 or 9) can be worked all in one color or in several colors; two colors can alternate, or variegated threads can be used with stunning effects. The designs can be enlarged, as needed.

10. Although not a traditional method of texturing, one closed geometric stitch can be repeated in rows of interlocking stitches to form a regular pattern on a patch. In spite of the fact that only one stitch is worked over and over again to create the design, the necessity for precise sizing and positioning of each individual stitch makes this the most difficult and time-consuming of the methods presented here. As you can see, the rows themselves need not interlock and may alternately reverse direction (Illus. 12-5). Execute with care and patience …

Illus. 12-3

Illus. 12-4

Illus. 12-5

Illus. 12-6

11. Some of our primary stitches can be used to cover a piece of cloth with a non-specific, rather organic-looking pattern. These may be worked on any crazyquilt fabric which might be improved by such designs. Preliminary marking would be very helpful but is optional. The first example shown in Illus. 12-6 is called threaded straight stitch and is found in "Stitches with Variations," a 40-page booklet by Jacqueline Enthoven (page 11). This is as much fun as any stitch you will ever try! Other possibilities include fern stitches, stem and backstitches, basic blanket, feather and chain stitches, and even spontaneously-worked arrowhead and Holbein stitches, randomly embellished with colonial knots or detached chain stitches.

12. Can you think of at least one noteworthy texturing technique that I have not covered? I must confess that the final method I will discuss did not occur to me until I made one last visit to my bookshelf. Upon leafing through Jan Eatons's beautiful revision of Mary Thomas's Dictionary of Embroidery Stitches, I found it: an entire chapter about needle-and-thread weaving and knotting over long, laid threads on small areas of cloth. To be sure, most of the 21 detached filling stitches presented by Ms. Eaton would not seem to be suitable for our purposes, largely because of their structural complexity, but also because none was ever used on an antique crazyquilt, to my knowledge. Even so, I must recommend four of these — namely, diamond filling stitch, battlement couching, two-color and multi-color surface darning, and plaited stitch. These stitcheries are not only easy to master, they are also very attractive. (See Eaton, pages 113 and 114, for color illustrations and instructions.)

Previously, I made reference to the time-honored crewelwork filling compositions which have been passed down through generations of enthusiasts, and which are documented in many fine books in several languages. The texturings we might add to our work are very reminiscent of those older, woolen-yarn applications. In fact, I have borrowed quite liberally from the past. The almost 2,200 embroidery designs presented in this book have been inspired by both the humble and the remarkable creations of people who made crazyquilts between 1860 and 1910 or so.

I cannot help but bless the extraordinary skill and ingenuity of those long-ago needle artists who gave us so many lovely stitch combinations and figurative motifs to contemplate and to use. Little could they imagine that, a century or more later, thousands of gentle women and men in a new millennium would consult their designs for possible inclusion in our work. Let us hope that our efforts may not only honor all of the gifted quiltmakers whose finished and almost-finished items we so admire, but that the "works of our hands" may also bring much pleasure and happiness to the eyes and lives of everyone who will one day encounter what we have wrought.

The Acknowledgments

In every human endeavor which helps to create a whole person in time and which advances the good and beautiful things in life, there are countless others who inspire, cheer, cajole, encourage, and, more often than not, directly assist the endeavorer in all her worthwhile achievements. Each of the following valued individuals knows what she did to fan the spark that enabled me to move beyond the many fears, uncertainties, and personal inadequacies I have long struggled against, until, amazingly, the enormity of the risks I must take in order to share my discoveries were overshadowed by the clarity of the path before me. To the extraordinarily generous "wonder women" of my long- and short-term acquaintance, my sincerest "thank you"! You could not possibly have known how much your unexpected but necessary acts of kindness would mean five, ten, and fifteen years down the road, or what your investments of time, shared information, and access to your quilts, shops, and stories would come to. It has all come to this — the book in your hands and the bettering of a self. May you, too, be blessed in ways unimagined!

THANK YOU, WITH ALL MY HEART:

Maureen McCarthy and the founding members of the Saint Cecilia's Cathedral Women's Guild and the Cathedral Quilting Circle, who gave me my first opportunity to teach quiltmaking to a large group; Joan Amato; Mary Lou Sherrerd, Merrilee Hansen, Dianne Duncan Thomas, Jennifer Perkins, Marjean Sargent, Linda Laine Banner, Pat Sears, Megan Legas; Sally Jo Holm; Lois Gottsch, Carol Uebner, Patty Kennedy, June Vogltance and her kind associates at Vogies Quilts & Treasures; and Karen Saemisch and the staff at Memory Lane Fabrics in Denison, Iowa; Lanna Galloway; Linda Cumbee, Tina Maruca, Frances Comfort, Jean Younkin, Shirley Hassler, and the Calico Quilt Club of Greater Columbus, Nebraska; Julie Strnad and "Baltimore Ladies and Laughter" (B.A.L.L.); the "Gone to Pieces" gals; Mary Barnett-Ramirez, Linda Novacek, Cindy Erickson, Betty Harmsen, Lorraine Fitzgerald, Betty Prochnow, Ila Chatfield, and Kay Labs; Mary Richling, Sara Sumnick Wamsat, Mandy Freiberg, Angela McLean, Renée Weinberg, Donna Stratker, Linda Konnath, Fay Kliewer, and Elaine Martin; Suzanne Earnest, Susan Seidel, Claudia Swee, Julie Prescott, Linda True, Janie Borg, Barbara Moore, Joyce Benitez, Lila Launer, Michelle Tech, and Marcia Nattrass; the Cottonwood Quilters of Nebraska; Wybeta Gilliam, Sue Gilliam, Mary Kay Green, Janice Zarestky, Arlene Wise,

AnnPauline McEvoy, Jean Tunink, Sandra Arnold, Carolyn Bailey, Sandra Eheman, Beth Nelson, and Katie Wilson; Teresa A. Martinek, Cinnamon Vrasper, Dallas L. Marshall, Bev Startzer, Beverly Burchfield, Donna Redding, and Miss Sara Miller of Kalona Kountry Kreations; Shelly Burge, Dr. Patricia Cox Crews, Sara Dillow, Laura Franchini, Brenda Groelz, Janice Lippincott, Jo Morton, Paulette Peters, Jenny Raymond, and Sharon Rexroad-Ericson; Mary Beth Jirsak, LeAnne Killion, Carol Brandl, Sally Mitchell, Ardis Wiese, Glenda Thompson, Emily Harris, and Eloise Thomsen. You represent the "tip of my iceberg" of people to whom I am indebted, along with Elinor Peace Bailey, Bonnie Browning, Christal Carter, Leslie Levison, Sue Linker, Jo Lischynski, Elly Sienkiewicz, and Anita Shackelford, who either taught needed skills to me or furthered my career in other substantial ways.

I wish to acknowledge the contributions made by the quilt owners, museum and historical-society officials, historians, and others without whose generosity and trust I could not have provided you with so many remarkable antique stitcheries and observations on this, our Joyous Undertaking. In order of acquaintance, I offer my deepest gratitude to these very kind people:

Rebecca A. Draper of Papillion, Nebraska, has a magnificent family crazyquilt dated 1870. It was made by her maternal great-great-grandmother, Kate Bowles Morris, in Paris, Tennessee. Becky very graciously gave me temporary custody of her treasure, but long enough to photograph it front and back and to draw nearly three pages of seamwork and patchwork stitcheries, several of which appear on pages 125, 164, and 180 (KBM).

Joan (pronounced Jo-Ann) Waldman of Platte Center, Nebraska, is a dear friend who also happens to be one of the most gifted of our state's quiltmakers. For 20 years she has designed original crazyquilt stitcheries in her spare time. To date she has imagined and drawn more than 10,000 gorgeous and whimsical motifs. She lent us two dozen of these for inclusion on pages 153, 154, and 159 (JLW).

Susan Jarosz of Omaha owns the quilt top from which I traced the Owl and the Cardinal on page 171. It is in nonrestorable condition but served an essential purpose here, as I do not know how to draw birds. Susie is widely known for her total mastery of practically every form of English and North American needlework, and she has a collection of related books and magazines rivaled only by the one held in the Library of Congress!

Dorothy Bond enthusiastically agreed in 1996 that I could copy primary stitches and embellishers directly from the 1,052 antique stitch combinations she documented in her landmark book, Crazy Quilt Stitches (self-published in 1981). The unadorned stitches are found throughout the Dictionary in Part

One and elsewhere in Part Two (CQS). As of this writing, Mrs. Bond's book is still in print and is available at quilt shops and from the author (34706 Row River Road / Cottage Grove OR 97424).

Doris Bowman and Virginia Eisemon welcomed me in October 1996 to their tiny crowded, but brightly cheerful offices at the Smithsonian Institution in Washington, D.C. They made me feel like a real research fellow, providing me with a work station of my own, complete with light table, slide projector, and access to all of the slides, transparencies, and curator's notes on every crazyquilt and embroidered quilt in the extensive collection. During that near-ecstatic visit, I hand-drew many stitcheries from the color slides. A splendid butterfly has been reproduced stitch-for-stitch on Page 168.

Penny McMorris of Bowling Green, Ohio, helped me to make sense of the copyright laws and public domain issues I had to address. Best of all, she enabled me to contact Catherine B. Shoe, heir to the exquisite Mittie Barrier Crazyquilt (see page 170). Ms. McMorris's book, Crazy Quilts (sadly out of print now), is still the best source of historical and design information we have on our subject in the English language.

Elizabeth Reinig of Panama, Iowa, insisted that I take home her museum-quality velvet and silk crazyquilt (circa 1900) to study and trace or draft the best patch pictures and line stitcheries for this book. The result: the first ten designs on page 105 and the wonderful floral tracings on pages 164, 165, and 166 (EBR). Betty is the first of all my former students to actually finish a large crazyquilt. Now, with her third one completed and three more in the planning, the pupil has become the teacher's teacher – in more ways than I can say.

Alice Hoffman did not hesitate to say "yes!" when I asked to use 42 straight-stitch designs (see pages 107, 108, 124, and 125 in the Treasury) from a heavily embroidered crazyquilt in the collection of the Museum of American Folk Art in New York (AFA). Initialed "S.H." and worked between 1885 and 1895, this gift of Margaret Cavigga (1985) appeared in America's Glorious Quilts and was featured on the dust jacket of that important book.

Amy Finkel of M. Finkel and Daughter, renowned antiques dealer of Philadelphia, Pennsylvania, also gave her approval to my including the Special Collection of stitcheries on page 106. The spectacular quilt from which they were drafted is now in private hands.

Robert Pettit of the Nebraska State Historical Society in Lincoln granted the needed go-ahead for the inclusion of the beautiful alphabet letter in Illus. 11-2 on page 200, as did Dr. Patricia Cox Crews, who co-edited the volume in which that partial monogram appears.

The Schuyler County Historical Society of Montour Falls, New York, has in its possession one of the most perfectly designed and worked crazyquilts I have ever seen. The one-of-a-kind spider's web on page 197 was closely copied (albeit not line for line) from this masterpiece, which was a bequest to the society by the Longnecker Estate circa 1973. This is the same quilt mentioned on page 56 as having the embroidered edges (flawlessly buttonhole-stitched), and I am indebted to Mrs. Shirley H. Craver for her willingness to share that lovely motif with all of us.

Virginia D. Kavvadias, branch manager at my favorite neighborhood library, provided more than occasional much-needed assistance during my many months of researching and drawing the designs for the patch pictures and spiders' webs chapters. Her genuine interest in the book and its progress was very much appreciated.

Virginia Welty, also of Lincoln, answered my letter for information by personally, unexpectedly, doing the research on a privately owned crazyquilt I wanted to include in the Treasury. She exemplifies the generous spirit of most people with whom I corresponded during the writing of the manuscript.

To everyone who made one of the blocks or quilts pictured herein, I say "Brava! Bellisima!" Your work makes the Treasury of Crazyquilt Stitches far more beautiful and instructive than it might otherwise have been. I thank Heaven for your friendship every day.

And Charlie, my incomparable husband, whose patient, constant love and support for 32 years have, quite literally, given the meaning to my life. For a long time, I have been in awe of his true goodness and his understanding of everything that matters. He makes me believe that Heaven is possible, even for me.

The Biography

Nebraska-born crazyquilt artist Carole Samples taught herself to sew on her grandmother's 1891 treadle machine when she was 12 years old. Her partnership with that temperamental relic resulted in a closet full of cotton dresses and nylon-net petticoats, and fostered an ever-growing appreciation of — and affection for — beautiful textiles.

Many years later as a new bride searching for decorating ideas at a local furniture store, Carole brought home the annual catalog which pictured an antique silk Log Cabin quilt in one of the room-setting photographs, and it changed her life forever. That one precious piece rekindled her early and long-dormant passion for fabric, which she began to collect with a vengeance as she shopped her way from Missouri to Maryland, from Pennsylvania to Vermont, and back home again during the U.S. Bicentennial years.

Like so many of us, Carole made scrap-look quilts in her three favorite palettes for about 14 years until, one day in the mid-1980s, she saw a fancy crazyquilt for the first time. The exact quilt and moment of discovery have long since escaped memory, but it was one of those definitive experiences which completely redirects the path one is upon. Now, 15 years later, Carole is recognized as one of the country's foremost experts on every aspect of traditional, nineteenth- and early twentieth-century crazyquilts, with particular emphasis on the thread and yarn embroidery applied to these quilts and their successors.

While mastering as many of the popular stitches as she could learn by herself, Carole reinvented the needlework sampler as a perfect vehicle for not only practicing and preserving new seamwork combinations as she discovered or imagined them, but also as the best device for teaching these same stitches to others of like sensibilities. This she has done since 1989, teaching diverse quiltmaking classes throughout Nebraska and in Iowa, offering seminars, retreats, and multi-session workshops through guilds, the Embroiderers' Guild of America's Omaha chapter, and through a community college in her home state. Along the way, she accepted several important commissions, the most noted of which is the National Park Service/Mid-west Regional Office's 75th Anniversary Fund-raising Quilt (see Quilter's Newsletter Magazine, April 1992).

Carole has been an active practitioner and promoter of this most eclectic form of patchwork as a founding member in 1994 of the Crazyquilters' Support Group of Eastern Nebraska. She was honored with an invitation to join the faculty of the American Quilter's Society's annual event in 1996, and that same year, she began in earnest to write the Treasury of Crazyquilt Stitches, her first book for AQS. To date, no fewer than 350 women owe to Carole the fact that they have gotten off to a proper start on the road to creating lovely items in old-style crazywork.

She continues to study and photograph crazyquilts wherever she finds them, drafting pages full of original and antique stitcheries for present and future velvet-and-lace people, and selling kits, patterns, threads, and related supplies through her tiny home-based company, fanCwerx. She dreams of one day establishing an international Registry of Crazyquilt Stitchery Designs and Motifs to which everyone who cares about the preservation of this marvelous artistic medium may contribute.

Carole and her galaxy-class husband, Charlie, summer and winter in Omaha.

Preliminary sketch of crazyquilt block, by the author, 1999

A Crazyquilter's Reading List

My list of excellent publications for crazy quilters of every skill level contains many favorites among the more than 250 titles I have collected over the years. Page numbers help to locate crazyquilt-related data and portraits in multiple-subject books. The books are classified by means of one or more Roman numerals which define each book's most significant contribution to the body of knowledge we makers of embellished items must consult from time to time. Numeral I means you will find a gallery of photographs, usually with a full vertical view of each crazyquilt and often accompanied by historical and descriptive notes both general and specific; II: there are projects and/or patterns featuring crazywork and related techniques; III: there are stitchery designs and, usually, instructions on how to make individual stitches in (A) thread and yarn, (B) ribbon, and/or (C) with punch needles; IV: there is at least one outstanding, stitchable alphabet worthy of our consideration; V: you will find outstanding graphic illustrations and other pictorial sources for patch decoration motifs; VI: other ornamental techniques are featured, such as appliqué, fabric dyeing, or basic quilt-construction methods, and the like.

A - Z of Embroidery Stitches, editor-in-chief, Margie Bauer (1997) ❧ III-A

Adventures in Stitches by Mariska Karasz (1949) ❧ III-A

American Patchwork & Quilting, edited by Gerald M. Knox (1985); pp. 80-93,166-167, 174, 205-207, 214-215, 229, 240-241, 247, 248, 270, 277-279, 281, 298-300, 310-311 ❧ I, II

The American Quilt/A History of Cloth and Comfort 1750 – 1950 by Roderick Kiracofe with Mary E. Johnson (1993); pp. vii, 146-149, 168-169, 171-172, 184-185,196, 206-208, 218-219, 234, 255 ❧ I

American Quilts and Coverlets in The Metropolitan Museum of Art by Amelia Peck (1990); pp. 88-99, 191 ❧ I

America's Glorious Quilts by Dennis Duke and Deborah Harding (1987); pp. 49, 54-55, 97, 131, 150-173, 185, 201, 276, 311 ❧ I

Antique Embroidery, compiled by Martha Campbell Pullen (1998) ❧ II, III-A,V

Appliqué Designs: My Mother Taught Me To Sew by Faye Anderson (1990) ❧ V, VI

The Beader's Companion by Judith Durant and Jean Campbell (1998) ❧ III-B

Butterflies: A Peterson Field Guide Coloring Book by Roger Tory Peteson, Robert Michael Pyle, and Sarah Anne Hughes, illustrator (1993) ❧ V

Butterfly Iron-On Transfer Patterns by Barbara Christopher (1991) ❧ V

Clues in the Calico: A Guide to Identifying and Dating Antique Quilts by Barbara Brackman (1989); pp. 36, 104-105, 107, 109-111, 121, 140,141, 143-146 ❧ I

The Complete Book of Crazy Patchwork by Mary Conroy (1985) ❧ (I), II, III-A

The Complete Guide to Embroidery Stitches and Crewel by Jo Bucher (1971) ❧ III-A

Crazy Patchwork and Quilting by Janet Haigh (1998) ❧ II, III-A, III-B

Crazy Quilt for Beginners by Machiko Miyatani ❧ II, III-A

Crazy Quilt Handbook by Judith Baker Montano (1986) ❧ I, II, III-A, III-C

Crazy Quilting/Heirloom Quilts/Traditional Motifs and Decorative Stitches by Christine Dabbs (1998) ❧ I, II, III-A, V

Crazy Quilt Odyssey/Adventures in Victorian Needlework by Judith Baker Montano (1991) ❧ I, II, III-A

Crazy Quilts by Penny McMorris (1984) ❧ I

Crazy Quilt Stitches by Dorothy Bond (1981) ❧ III-A

Crazy Rags by Deborah Brunner (1996) ❧ II, III-A, III-B

Creative Crazy Patchwork by Helen Moore and Theresia Stockton (1997) ❧ II, III-A, III-B

Daddy's Ties by Shirley Botsford (1995) ❧ II, VI

Decorative Initials Iron-On Transfers by Mary C. Waldrep (1993) ❧ IV

Dimensional Appliqué/Baskets, Blooms, & Baltimore Borders by Elly Sienkiewicz (1993); pp. 11-71 ❧ II, VI, (III-A)

Elegant Stitches/An Illustrated Guide and Source Book of Inspiration by Judith Baker Montano (1995) ❧ III-A, III-B, VI

The Encyclopedia of Embroidery Techniques by Pauline Brown (1994) ❧ III-A, III-B, VI

Forget Me Not/A Gallery of Friendship and Album Quilts by Jane B. Kolter (1985); pp. 87-95, 99, 111 ❧ I

A Gallery of Amish Quilts/Design Diversity from a Plain of People by Robert Bishop and Elizabeth Safanda (1976); pp. 54-55 ❧ I

Glorious American Quilts by Elizabeth V. Warren & Sharon L. Eisenstat (1996); pp. 72-87 ❧ I

How To Make An Old-fashioned Crazy Quilt by J.M. Mischler (revised 1993) ❧ II

Ideas & Inspirations/A Punchneedle Techniques Primer by Marinda Stewart (1985) ❧ III-C

J. & P. Coats' 100 Embroidery Stitches/Book 150-B (1979) ❧ III-A

Kate Greenway Iron-On Transfer Patterns by Julie Hassler (1990) ❧ V

The Magic of Crazy Quilting by J. Marsha Mischler (1998) ❧ I, III-A, III-B; IV, V, VI

Mary Thomas's Dictionary of Embroidery Stitches (revised edition) by Jan Eaton (1989); pp. 6-9, 12-77, 82-114 ❧ III-A

Nebraska Quilts & Quiltmakers, edited by Patricia C. Crews & Ronald C. Naugle (1991); pp. 114, 117, 123, 137, 141, 142-165 ❧ I

North Carolina Quilts, edited by Ruth Haislip Roberson (1988); pp. ❧ I

Old-Fashioned Floral Iron-On Transfer Patterns by Mary Carolyn Waldrep (1993) ❧ IV, V

The Quilt Encyclopedia Illustrated by Carter Houck; pp. 54-55, 62, 64, 73, 116, 152-153, 170-171, 177-179, 186 ❧ I

Quilts Galore! by Laura Nownes and Diana McClun (1990); pp. 105-116 ❧ II, VI, (III-A)

Quilt Treasures of Great Britain by Janet Rae, Margaret Tucker, et al. (1993); pp. 9, 11, 12, 56-57, 58-59, 62, 136-137, 151, 154-155, 161, 162, 166, 168 ❧ I

Reader's Digest Complete Book of Embroidery by Melinda Coss
(1996) ⚹ II, III-A, -B, IV, V
The Red Book by Diane Arthurs (1998) ⚹ III-A, V

Small Endearments/Nineteenth-Century Quilts for Children and Dolls
(second edition, revised and expanded 1994); pp. 107, 121, 123-125,
130-131, 139, 150 ⚹ I
The Stitches of Creative Embroidery by Jacqueline Enthoven
(1964) ⚹ III-A

The Timeless Art of Embroidery by Helen Stevens (1997) ⚹ III-A
*Three-Dimensional Appliqué and Embroidery/Techniques for Today's
Album Quilt* by Anita Shackelford (1994) ⚹ V, VI, (III-A)

Victorian Elegance by Lezette Thomason (1996) ⚹ II, III-A
Victorian Patchwork and Quilting by Arlene Dettore and Beverly
Maxvill (1995) ⚹ II, III-A

Wrapped in Glory: Figurative Quilts & Bedcovers 1700 – 1900 by Sandi
Fox (1990); pp. 10, 12, 128-131, 146-149, 154-157, 158-161, 162-165 ⚹ I,V

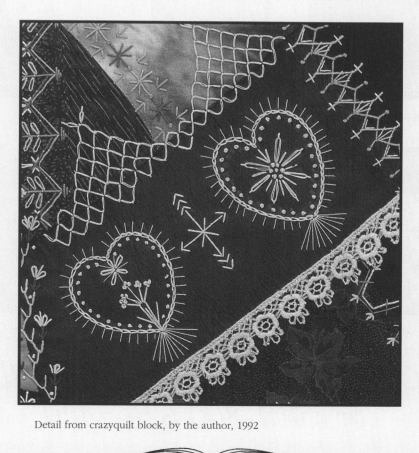

Detail from crazyquilt block, by the author, 1992

This is only a small selection of the books available from the American Quilter's Society. AQS books are known worldwide for timely topics, clear writing, beautiful color photos, and accurate illustrations and patterns. The following books are available from your local bookseller, quilt shop, or public library.

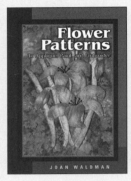

#5238 • $19.95

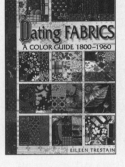

#4827 • $24.95

#3788 • $24.95

#2380 • $9.95

#4833 • $14.95

#5331 • $16.95

#5175 • $24.95

#5140 • $14.95

#4593 • $24.95

Look for these books nationally or call 1-800-626-5420

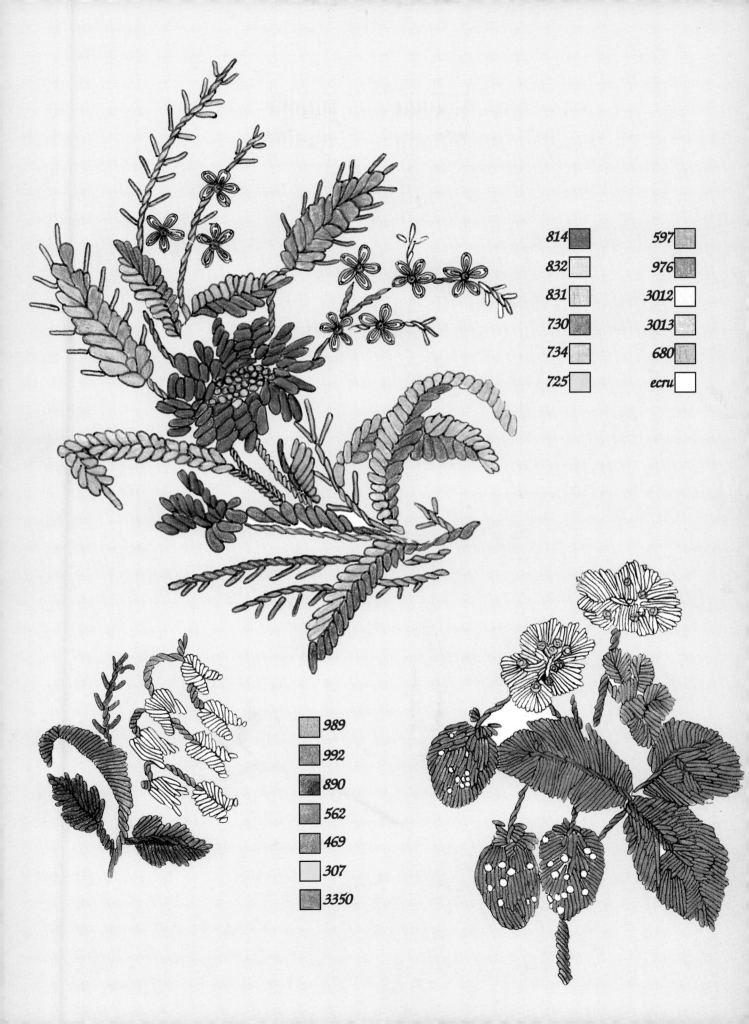

814
832
831
730
734
725

597
976
3012
3013
680
ecru

989
992
890
562
469
307
3350